The Power in Compassion

Transforming the Correctional Culture

By Vicki Sanderford-O'Connor

Published in the United States by O'Connor's Enterprises, Inc., Fair Oaks, California

For information on this book contact
Vicki Sanderford-O'Connor:

Designing solutions, strategy and
change through people

P.O. Box 1717, Fair Oaks, CA 95628
Phone 916-961-5394
Email vicki@clariquest.com
www.clariquest.com

ISBN 0-9706071-0-5

Printed in the United States of America

Editing: WordSpring Writing Consultants

Cover and book design: Mystic Design, Inc.

Photographs: PhotoDisc, Inc. and Jack Rhyne

Table of Contents

Introduction

I always thought that it would be an inmate or parolee who took me out, not the stress. After sixteen years in the California Department of Corrections, I suffered a stress-induced heart attack. One minute I had an exciting career and national visibility; the world seemed promising. The next I thought I was going to die. Suffice it to say it was a defining moment in my life. Three days later I was at home, extremely frightened and wondering if I was going to live. I began, as many do, to reflect on my life, my career, and my family. This book is a result of that reflection.

My life and the lives of my family have been entwined with the Department. I began my career as a Medical Technical Assistant in 1982 before moving on to the classification of Parole Agent in 1987, and culminating in 1999 as Parole Agent III, Community Correctional Program Manager, with oversight of multiple, community-based programs and a $14 million dollar budget.

My family has been impacted by the system in ways I would never have anticipated. My eldest son spent many years as an inmate and parolee; my youngest son recently graduated from the California Department of Corrections, correctional officer-training academy. Each son's experience within the system has added or helped shape my perception of Corrections.

When my youngest son told me that he would be attending the Academy, I determined that I would give him the information that he needed:

- To work successfully within the system;

- To maintain his health by addressing up front those issues that contribute to the stress of the profession, such as managing the effects of evil, fear and politics, which are not addressed in any classroom of which I am aware; and

- To maintain the integrity of his family.

Upon drafting these letters, I determined that my son would not be working in a vacuum, and there are many others who could benefit from a mother-yet-seasoned-warrior's best wisdom on the correctional culture. With permission from my sons, I have determined to publish the letters to this end:

- To increase the likelihood of my brothers and sisters in corrections successfully maneuvering the system and to alert them to the suffering the stress of the system can produce;

- To open a dialogue on the taboo subjects of fear, violence, evil, politics, hate, and weakness;

- To affirm that the effects of correctional officer stress: alcoholism; substance addiction; suicide; officer violence and misconduct; high divorce rates; health issues such as cardiac events, high blood pressure, and strokes can be reduced by creating an approach to work that is holistic; and

- To validate the experiences and professionalism of those who work the system.

This book is not about sensationalism nor is it an academic dissertation; it is about realities and truth. I attempt to share my experiences without bias and anger, but the reality is we see the world through a filtered lens. It is my intent that this book will begin to heal an ailing system, a system in denial, and through my voice, others will be spared the fear and pain of a near-death experience and the defeating, demeaning Worker's Compensation process. If this book spares even one person, than I have done my job.

The Author

Vicki Sanderford-O'Connor
Correctional Consultant and Trainer

Vicki knows how to get the job done. She's been widely recognized as a tough-minded, clear thinker, and she doesn't mind shaking up the house. In 1996, Vicki was honored as the "Best in the Business" in *Corrections Today*. The California Probation, Parole and Correctional Association named Vicki "Parole Agent of the Year." It was Vicki Sanderford-O'Connor who developed and managed implementation of what became the second program introduced in CDC history that successfully reduced recidivism and saved taxpayer dollars. She built her 16-year career in California's prison system tackling core issues related to its organizational culture. Moving up through the ranks, Vicki knows first hand the issues faced daily by those inside the institution, on both sides of the bars.

"She's not in it for her ego. She's in it to help the system work better," says Fran Berkowitz, former CDC administrator. She's put her heart into her work, and she still does. Following a stress-related heart attack in 1998 that ended her career within the prison system, Vicki transformed and expanded her approach. "This is a passion for me – not a job," Vicki noted in *Corrections Today* (October 1996). Now she's available to share her wisdom and experience with others working in institutions. She knows how to:

Photo by Jack Rhyne

- **Raise awareness and stimulate a dialogue;**

- **Distinguish between the symptoms and the causes of a fractured organizational culture;**

- **Facilitate the development of organizational vision and articulate that vision in workable strategy; and**

- **Work backward from the desired future to create action plans that overcome problems, change behaviors, and alleviate ongoing external pressures.**

In presentations to diverse groups, Vicki uses stories from the trenches to raise awareness about the prison culture and environment. She takes her message to conferences, conventions, and community groups. She encourages action and involvement, and inspires in others what she lives every day, a "passion for action." With each presentation, she creates new converts to her methods. Among her greatest strengths is her ability to talk to new correctional officers and managers, to convey what she learned firsthand: that change and improvement begin within. Start by changing yourself if you want to thrive, instead of merely survive. "You learn how to feed your heart; how to fight fiercely for what you know is right." "And soon," Vicki points out, "You're not one of the many. That's the surprising thing. People learn that compassion is not fluffy or soft. You have to be willing and ready to trust your intuition – and that's scary. It's not for the faint at heart."

The Facts

Did you know that California has the third-largest prison system in the world (after China and the U.S. as a whole)? For $4.6 billion for the 1999/2000 fiscal year, Californian taxpayers fund a dangerous, even deadly prison environment, where fear stalks correctional officers and inmates alike.

And fear exacts a high toll, beyond physical injuries and death. It fosters the growth of a culture of violence; it instigates misconduct and promotes cover-ups of wrongdoing. At the same time, correctional staff members learn to cover up their emotional reactions, they lose their sense of appropriate boundaries and, as a result, they experience debilitating emotional problems. Disabling stress is often manifested in high turnover rates, alcoholism, substance abuse, marital problems, and other issues. The toll on families and loved ones is incalculable (*Peacekeeper*, March/April 2000).

Both violence turned outward as misconduct toward inmates and violence turned inward as self-destructive behavior cost taxpayers tens of millions of dollars each year. In 1997, for example, litigation by inmates alleging excessive force and other misconduct cost taxpayers approximately $35 million.

Clearly there are problems with the current situation, problems that thus far proved difficult to manage. **Well, I can help save millions** of dollars each year by introducing new tools for sound decision-making, through a series of workshops, training seminars, meeting facilitation, executive coaching and consulting to police and corrections professionals, policy makers and private security organizations.

I demonstrate how the skills and behavioral tools of breakthrough thinking, emotional intelligence, and Discerning Follower-ship™ can be adapted to the reality of the corrections environment to reduce costs related to stress disability claims, poor labor relations, litigation associated with alleged officer misconduct. I train correctional professionals and law enforcement and security officers on how to use these

practical tools in situations they encounter every day on the job.

Only by beginning at last to address these problems, can we hope to improve this situation. The purpose of my work is to improve prison conditions on both sides of the bars, for inmates and for correctional staff and, in doing so:

- **Set a new standard for staff behavior based on emotional intelligence and on the power of compassion in the correctional environment.**

- **Offer alternative methods to reduce stress, address conflict, and manage emotions.**

- **Add to the decision-making tools COs adopt in inmate interactions.**

- **Decrease litigation related to charges of correctional officer misconduct.**

- **Reduce increased costs due to poor labor relations.**

- **Cut the number of stress disability claims against the CDC.**

- **Improve morale and strengthen ethical awareness.**

- **Help correctional staff see the institutional culture differently.**

- **Ultimately, to change the correctional culture from one in which violence and aggression are routine into one in which the environment is safer and saner for both inmates and staff.**

THE PURPOSE OF MY WORK IS TO IMPROVE PRISON CONDITIONS ON BOTH SIDES OF THE BARS, FOR INMATES AND FOR CORRECTIONAL STAFF. . .

No institution changes over night. Explosive growth over the past two decades has made it possible for entrenched problems to become routine. Now is the time to address these problems. If these issues are left unresolved, correctional costs will continue to escalate as will increased legislative and media scrutiny and court intervention. It is time for Correctional Professionals to take the initiative for cultural change.

THE CALIFORNIA PRISON SYSTEM

- **California has the third-largest prison system in the world,** following China and the U.S. as a whole (Mike Davis, "Hell factories in the field: A prison-industrial complex," *The Nation*, Feb. 20, 1995:229).

- **With an annual budget of $4.6 billion (1999/2000 Budget Act), California taxpayers support 33 state prisons, 38 minimum-custody camps and 8 prison-mother facilities; current prison population: 160,846 inmates**
  (CDC Facts, California Dept. of Corrections [CDC], Second Quarter, 2000).

- **Average yearly cost per inmate: $21, 243.** (This cost is probably understated: see "California Department of Corrections," State Auditor Report #97215, Sept. 1998, which found that CDC understated per-inmate annual costs by $3,795, when it failed to include over $400 million in capital costs, $15 paid to local governments and $84 million in the department's share of state overhead. In all, CDC costs were understated by more than $500 million. The audit found that costs varied considerably from prison to prison, from as low as $18,562 to as high as $38,554 per year.)

- **Since the 1980s, CDC has undertaken the largest prison-building program in the U.S.,** at a cost of $5.27 billion; by April, 2004, according to CDC projections, the inmate population will exceed available capacity of 177,197 (CDC Facts, California Dept. of Corrections [CDC], Second Quarter, 2000).

- **Current staff totals 45,976, including 39,761 in Institutions, 2,912 in Parole and 3,086 in Administration** (CDC Facts, California Dept. of Corrections [CDC], Second Quarter, 2000).

- **Current number of felons under CDC jurisdiction: 304,032**
  (CDC Facts, California Dept. of Corrections [CDC], Second Quarter, 2000).

- **Purpose: "operates all state prisons, oversees a variety of community correctional facilities, and supervises all parolees during their re-entry into society."**
  (CDC Facts, California Dept. of Corrections [CDC], Second Quarter, 2000).

WITH AN ANNUAL BUDGET OF $4.6 BILLION, CALIFORNIA TAXPAYERS SUPPORT A CURRENT PRISON POPULATION OF 160,846 INMATES

- **Who gets locked up?**

Race/ethnicity:		
	93% males	7% females
	34% Hispanic	31% black
	29% white	5% other
Offense:	43% persons	28% drugs
	22% property	6% other

("CDC Facts," California Dept. of Corrections [CDC], Second Quarter, 2000).

THE CULTURE OF VIOLENCE

- **Violence is deeply rooted in the California prison system;** even at the California Youth Authority (CYA), "many wards live ... in constant fear of physical attacks from other wards and retaliation from staff" *(Sacramento Bee, 5/17/00).*

- **California correctional officers are assaulted by inmates, on average, more than seven times each day** according to the California Department of Corrections, which reports 2,606 inmate attacks on correctional officers (COs) at the State's 33 prisons during 1999 *(Sacramento Bee, 5/28/00).*

- **Violence works both ways.** As the Legislative Analysts' Office put it, "The CDC has been plagued by serious allegations ... [of] excessive force and, in some cases, deadly violence against inmates...." *(1997/98 Budget Analysis,* Legislative Analysts' Office, 1997:1)

"YOU DON'T GIVE IT THAT MUCH THOUGHT.... YOU NEVER THINK IT'S GOING TO BE YOU. YOU JUST KIND OF SWALLOW THAT SICK GUT FEELING YOU MIGHT HAVE."

- **Use of excessive force.** COs get "used to" the violence. "You don't give it that much thought.... You never think it's going to be you. You just kind of swallow that sick gut feeling you might have." Says Folsom Prison CO Bob Buda, after being slashed by an inmate during a routine prisoner escort *(Sacramento Bee, 5/28/00).*

- **Violence doesn't excuse CO misconduct**–including inciting violence–nor does it condone the cover-ups investigators routinely encounter. (A task force investigation formed by the Dept.. of Corrections in Nov. 1996 confirmed 13 cases of cover ups in incidents related to CO misconduct and aggression, including staged fights. (Noted in an editorial, "Who guards the guards?" *Orange County Register,* 6/3/98; see also *LA Times* articles for much greater detail on cover-up and limitations on investigation set by both Department and attorney general's office).

- **Legislative Analysts' Office recommendations for reform of long-standing personnel problems within CDC:**

  ~ Improve quality and training of correctional personnel.

  ~ Make sure supervisory personnel who have moved up quickly during the great expansion of the prison system have adequate and appropriate managerial training.

~ Once recruitment/training goals are reached, redirect training funds to focus on mid-level managers and to expand CO candidates with psychological training. (*1997/98 Budget Analysis*, Legislative Analysts' Office, 1997:8)

WAGES OF VIOLENCE AND MISCONDUCT

• **Inmate litigation.** Lawsuits filed by inmates and correctional personnel expected to reach $35 million in 1997; a 14 percent increase in two years. ("Correctional litigation a growing fiscal issue," *1997/98 Budget Analysis*, Legislative Analysts' Office, 1997:2)

• **During 1991/96 at Corcoran (alone), inmates filed an average of about 800 to 1,000 lawsuits** each year, according to Dan Lundgren. *LA Times*

INMATE LITIGATION. LAWSUITS FILED BY INMATES AND CORRECTIONAL PERSONNEL EXPECTED TO REACH $35 MILLION IN 1997

I Can't Believe You Are in the Correctional Officer Academy

October 27, 1999

Dear Tony:

I t hit me emotionally today, as I knew it eventually would, that you are actually in the Correctional Officer Academy and, in six weeks, if you find that corrections is in fact your calling, you will be assigned to San Quentin. Until today, the possibility of your employment with the California Department of Corrections had only been an abstract thought for me – just one of several careers you were considering that would give you the means to fulfill yourself and to provide for your family. I know that in a sense, you were raised within the correctional system because of my employment. You learned a lot through the stories and the experiences I shared over the years. You also watched and learned from your brother's incarceration. As a result of your observations, you learned to make sound decisions in your life. You faced a variety of options, including the road your brother chose because of his addictions. I am pleased and proud that you chose to follow in my footsteps into corrections. You need to understand, however, that footsteps will only take you to the gate.

Tony, you will forge your own trail within the system. It's a challenging system that is at once fun, exciting, and full of opportunities. Multiple career paths wait. They will become evident as you mature in the system. Expect to make close friends and to develop camaraderie with your fellow officers beyond what you have experienced in any other job. A whole new world awaits you. But you are behind the eight ball from the moment you begin.

Winifred Gallagher, in her book *The Power of Place* describes the powerful influence that the environment has on our emotions, either positive or negative. Corrections is a negative environment, a world that is rife with danger, complexity, fear, and violence. That's why I have

chosen to give you all the information I can to raise your awareness and to help you develop tools to counteract the effects of this negative environment so you can succeed and to keep you safe. Let me explain.

While I worked in corrections, when people found out what I did for a living, they always commented that I must be brave. My mother knew better when she responded that I wasn't brave, I just didn't have much common sense. Tony, your grandmother may be smarter than she realizes. I accepted a position in corrections in 1982, but I did not have a clue about what I was getting into. When I went into the institution, the Correctional Medical Facility in Vacaville, I had to learn very quickly how to survive. Coworkers who failed to apply common sense either lost their jobs by becoming an unwitting ally to an inmate or by aligning themselves with misdirected staff. Still others left due to injuries received in the line of duty. I learned many lessons during my 16-year tenure; in some instances, I learned the hard way. Over time, through listening and observation, I found my own path and honed my survival instincts. I achieved a measure of success and felt as though I made a difference. I would like to say that I made it out of the system safely, unscathed by ill effects of the negative culture, but we both know that isn't true, as evidenced by my heart attack.

YOU WILL WORK IN A DANGEROUS ENVIRONMENT, WHERE COMPLACENCY PRESENTS THE BIGGEST DANGER. AS YOU KNOW, THE EFFECTS OF THE JOB-RELATED STRESS ALMOST KILLED ME.

My first instinct is to protect you. Working in corrections was okay for me. It was my choice. I reaffirmed that decision daily because it was the most fulfilling work I have ever performed. Now that you have chosen this same path, I know what it feels like to have a person you love working in the system. I am concerned for you, as deeply concerned as I felt about your brother when he became an inmate. I am concerned because I know what can happen, I learned to recognize the landmines, and I have been injured and scarred in the process. You will work in a dangerous environment, where complacency presents the biggest danger. As you know, the effects of the job-related stress almost killed me. I have also seen the effects of the stress on others, many of them friends: alcoholism; depression; suicide; substance abuse; divorce; and myriad health concerns, including ulcers, high blood pressure, strokes, and cardiac problems.

I have to respect your choice of career, as I demanded others respect my choice when they voiced concern. So, I decided to try and protect you the only way I know how, by giving you information. I have thought long and hard about the most critical elements that lead a per-

son to success within corrections, not just the skills and abilities they teach in the Academy, but also those behaviors, thoughts, and actions peculiar to the correctional culture, significant issues that I never heard anyone talk about or acknowledge in any training curriculum. While you attend the Academy, I plan to share information that I wish someone would have shared with me when I went through training. These personal views and observations were gleaned from my experience working in corrections, along with insights developed through my curiosity and voracious reading from other fields, through formal education and finally the wisdom and lessons learned from life. This is not intended to be an academic dissertation; it is about my perception of realities and truth.

First of all, I want to give you my personal success equation. This formula has served me well over the years. I have found that the elements in the success equation allow a person to succeed in any situation: at work, in their social lives, or in relationships with other people. Next, I will prove to you that there is **Power** in Compassion and that **genuine** caring and **genuine** concern are legitimate tools for your arsenal of skills in managing people.

I WILL PROVE TO YOU THAT THERE IS POWER IN COMPASSION AND THAT **GENUINE** CARING AND **GENUINE** CONCERN ARE LEGITIMATE TOOLS FOR YOUR ARSENAL OF SKILLS IN MANAGING PEOPLE.

Later on, I will introduce you to the concept of "Discerning Follower-ship™," the ability to perceive or recognize that something is different from the norm, measuring that difference against the yardstick of right values and principals and then to consciously decide whether to follow or resist. Discerning Follower-ship™ is a skill so important that I will devote an entire letter to the subject. I also want you to be able to recognize the face of evil, to know that evil displays itself in many deceitful, compelling ways. There are methods for recognizing and combating evil including anchoring and holding fast to the right values and principles and using them as a guide in decision making.

Beyond that, I want to talk to you about intuition and fear – both healthy attributes. You will soon learn the great cultural taboo not to show weakness in any form or fashion. This cultural phenomenon has been distorted to the detriment of your health and emotional well-being. I want you to understand the power of lateral influence in shaping the culture. Doing your job to the best of your ability means awareness of politics and of the danger of being "in the car" when cars break down. I want you, above all, to be a leader so I'll tell you what I've learned about leadership by modeling.

At the same time, knowing the value of using your family as a "barometer," as a measure of the impact of the system on your emotional well-being and relationships with others is significant. Finally, I want to share constructive strategies to help you avoid complacency, to maintain your health and wellness, and to manage stress.

Some of this information you already know and these letters will only serve as a reminder; some information will trigger your thinking and allow you to center yourself as you step into your future. Most of all I want you to be happy, successful, healthy, and balanced and safe. You have a family to care for and who cares for you.

I know maneuvering the hiring process has been a long, hard road, and I congratulate you on your success in doing so. I want you to know I love you, and I am proud of the way you have taken charge of your life. You are a good person, son and father, and a loving husband, and soon you will be an excellent Correctional Officer.

MOST OF ALL I WANT YOU TO BE HAPPY, SUCCESSFUL, HEALTHY, AND BALANCED AND SAFE.

Until next time,
Love Mom

CHAPTER 2

The Success Equation

November 3, 1999

Dear Tony,

I saw your wife (Kim) and your sons yesterday. Anthony had another earache. The doctor gave him some medicine, and he is doing better already. Devante wanted his mom to cut his hair, and Kim was tired from working. All and all, things are pretty much the same. I am going to Anthony's school with the storyteller on the nineteenth of this month. That will be so much fun. Speaking of stories, I have one for you today.

The biggest lie I was ever told, and the biggest myth that separates people from success in this lifetime is: "If you are smart, you can do anything and be anything that you like." I heard this saying at a very early age and actually believed it for years. It seems to imply that you need not add anything to your arsenal, that if you use your intelligence, answers will automatically come to you.

As I matured, I met many bright people who were not successful. Many bright people seem to lack the qualities necessary to achieve their dreams. I was one of those people for a time. For years I just went along doing my best. I graduated from high school, married, and waited for success to arrive on my doorstep. I was smart and, according to the formula I had been given, I should be leading a happy, fulfilled life. I wasn't. Sometimes your life experiences do not equate with the "truths" given to you as a child.

I recently attended a Platform Skills Lab, hosted by the National Speakers Association, in Phoenix, Arizona. The purpose of the lab was to help speakers in honing their speaking/presentation skills. The theme of the lab was baseball, and each of the nine workshops had a catchy title that corresponded with that theme: "Stretching Exercise: Unbend Your Mind"; "Great Openers: How to Knock the Opening Pitch out of the Ballpark"; and "Audience Involvement: Getting the Crowd in

the Game." I learned a lot in each of those workshops, and I also got confirmation that what is taught is not always correct.

A very bright woman, Janelle M. Barlow, Ph.D., discussed the cultural practice in China of binding women's feet. Apparently, this practice began when a dancer in the Emperor's Court tied back her toe to create an enticing shadow while she was dancing. The practice caught on and resulted in the cruel binding of girl's feet. Each woman determined when her feet were bound, that when she had daughters, she would not inflict the same painful practice. They bound their daughters' feet anyway. Janelle cited this cultural phenomenon to demonstrate the power of the teaching we received as children, the power of culture. For me, the bottom line in her workshop was that to be creative, we needed to loosen the bindings of the "truths" we had been taught. We need to recapture our free-spirited youth, to reexamine old "truths" and to think "out of the box" if we want to build successful speaking business or, for that matter, any successful career or life. It struck me then that I had to overcome 50 years of mind-conforming behavior, the sort of behavior I had fought as a child, as I struggled to hold on to my individuality, and rightfully so.

> AS I MATURED AND OBSERVED PEOPLE, I FOUND THAT INTELLIGENCE GUARANTEED NOTHING. I MET HIGHLY EDUCATED PEOPLE WHO WORKED LONG HOURS FOR LOW PAY AT UNFULFILLING, DEAD-END JOBS THAT THEY HATED.

What does this story have to do with the myth of "being smart?" How does it translate into career or life success? As I matured and observed people, I found that intelligence guaranteed nothing. I met highly educated people who worked long hours for low pay at unfulfilling, dead-end jobs that they hated. Gradually, I discovered the real success equation:

1. **You must be intelligent and motivated enough to pursue technical proficiency;**

2. **You must know yourself; and**

3. **You must have empathy for the other person.**

It may surprise you to learn that, in my experience, technical proficiency accounts for only one third of the equation; knowing yourself and having empathy for others are equally important, and all must be in balance. You will hold many different roles in life and not all situations you will encounter call for the same skill level or response. Some situations you encounter in the institution may call for technical proficiency. Others times your wisdom, principals, and empathy for the person you are dealing with will guide you. Surviving within the institution walls and in life will take grounding in all of these areas.

TECHNICAL SKILLS

At the Academy you learn the rules of the game and like most games there is a strategy. What you learn at the Academy is only the beginning of your education, and keep in mind technical skills are only one third of the success equation. Corrections is a vast field, with so many rules and regulations governing the administration of an institution that you cannot learn everything you need to know during six weeks of Academy training. Learn the rules, and play within the boundaries of those rules. Such policies and procedures will protect you from disciplinary and legal problems. Ask the officers at Corcoran prison who got caught up in the sweeping investigations surrounding alleged inmate brutality incidents that made front-page news for so long. Those officers who worked within the parameters of the Standard Operating Procedures withstood the scrutiny they came under.

> YOUR BEST DEFENSE IS TO ALWAYS DO YOUR JOB WITHIN THE CONFINES OF ESTABLISHED POLICY AND DOCUMENT YOUR ACTIONS THOROUGHLY.

You told me an officer already employed within the Department suggested you purposefully downplay your shooting skill. They said that if you were ever in a position in where you had to use your weapon, and you made a mistake, your solid shooting record on the range would work to your detriment. I do not know that I agree with that advice. Unfortunately, defensive posturing is the name of the game in corrections. Inmates are litigious, as are inmates' rights groups. Some members of the legislature have left no stone unturned in investigations of alleged wrongdoing. They are looking for the perpetrators and will not hesitate to use you as an example, if you give them opportunity, if you do not follow policy and procedure.

Trust me, if you stay in corrections, there will come a time when you are called on to defend a disciplinary that you have issued, give a deposition in a court case, or testify on the witness stand. Your best defense is to always do your job within the confines of established policy and document your actions thoroughly. Listen to your instructors. They have been there and you will benefit from their experience. Along with technical knowledge, however, you must know yourself.

KNOW YOURSELF

Knowing yourself accounts for another third of the success equation. Knowing yourself includes being anchored to your values, your goals, and your purpose in life, which includes the spiritual as well as the secular purpose, and it involves understanding and managing your

emotions. Trust me: this may seem basic, but nowhere is it more important that you be anchored to a moral code, spiritually fit, guided by sound principles and emotionally grounded than in the correctional environment. This environment can be hopeless, violent, and indifferent. Everything you know and believe will be challenged. You will be confronted by every sort of evil and deprivation – sometimes wrapped in sheep's clothing, sometimes disguised so well the stories can become compelling.

Working in this environment can slowly poison people who are not alert. It is insidious. Without strong roots in your beliefs and principles, if you are not doing something in your personal life to offset your experiences at work, you will lose your direction. I know. Two years into my career with the California Department of Corrections, working at the California Medical Facility in Vacaville as an Medical Technical Assistant, I was involved in an incident that forced me to look at myself and face my own callousness and indifference.

I SAW EVERYTHING. I KNEW WHAT THE INMATES WERE CAPABLE OF DOING TO EACH OTHER: STABBINGS, BEATINGS, BROKEN LIMBS, MUTILATIONS, AND RAPE.

I had worked in the B1 Clinic for two years, and I loved the action. It was the hub of medical care for the entire facility. Almost everything that happened medically was filtered through that clinic: sick call, administration of medication, emergency/trauma room, alarm response, ambulance, and just about anything else that involved medical necessity. I saw it all, and I bought into the culture of the system very quickly.

I was not weak. I handled whatever they threw at me, and I developed a strong camaraderie with my brother and sister correctional officers: we were in it together. Whatever happened to one of them happened to me. My responsibility on the team was to manage the medical details of the job, and if another staffer got hurt in the course of performing their duties, to get them treated and safely home.

I bought into the negative culture of the system, and it happened insidiously. Over the course of two years of action, I saw everything. I knew what the inmates were capable of doing to each other: stabbings, beatings, broken limbs, mutilations, and rape. I had no illusions about what they would do to me or my brothers or sisters if given the opportunity. One day it happened.

An inmate stabbed an officer. I remember that day vividly because it brought home to me the truth that this game was real. It is difficult for me to explain. How I got angry and I wanted to take it out on every inmate in the institution. I felt, "How dare they?" I knew that the whole population had not stabbed the officer but I looked at them as a whole. I hated all of "them." This is the day I bought into the culture; it was "us versus them." As little incidents occurred, the poison within me grew, until I had what I call my "great awakening."

A shooting occurred at Solano, a new prison back then. The populations in their yards were different than the population in the medical facility. The mission and programs of the facility were different, and consequently they had different problems. That day we received the call that Solano had "a man down" and that he was being transported to our clinic. We were already prepared for anything. Responding to trauma was a daily event for my unit.

The man, victim of a gunshot wound to the heart, was dead on arrival, one causality of a huge fight between rival gangs in the yard. This is not unusual in and of itself. What made it unusual for me was that this was the first shooting by a staff member, which I was involved in and which I had the opportunity to observe the staff's response. I observed no consternation, no one appeared upset. In fact one of the female officers sang "One Less Egg to Fry" and we all joined in on the chorus. The officer, who had shot the inmate, drank a cup of coffee and was ready to go back up in the tower and resume his duties.

...ONE OF THE FEMALE OFFICERS SANG "ONE LESS EGG TO FRY"... THE OFFICER, WHO HAD SHOT THE INMATE, DRANK A CUP OF COFFEE AND WAS READY TO GO BACK UP IN THE TOWER AND RESUME HIS DUTIES.

Do not get me wrong, you must do your job, and there may come a time when during a narrowly defined set of circumstances, you must shoot and possibly kill another human being. But *my reaction* to the situation horrified me; facing it without a cringe, without regard for human life, and without anger at the wasted potential of this person, borders on criminal in my mind. What separates a free man from the person who is locked up? Isn't it feelings, empathy, moral standards? This incident was so traumatic for me; that it shook me to the depths of my being. I had to rethink my position.

I went home that night and took a good look at myself in the mirror and realized I had lost my center, the very core of my existence. I had to answer some tough questions and clarify my values.

WHY HAD I CHOSEN CORRECTIONS?

- Did the brutal environment numb my emotions and if so, how was I to prevent that from occurring again?

- Were the pay and benefits worth the loss of my ability to experience my own emotions?

- Had I allowed the seeds of negativity from my workplace to sprout in my home and if so, how could I repair the damage and prevent it from occurring again?

- Was my job worth exchanging for a lifetime, because I only have one?

- Was I making a difference or making a living?

- How did my work contribute to a better world?

- What would be my legacy if I continued to work in Corrections?

- If I chose to stay, how could I regain my balance and maintain a healthy perspective?

I BEGAN TO MANAGE MY EMOTIONS, ACTING ON THE INFORMATION THEY GAVE ME INSTEAD OF REACTING. I WANTED TO MAKE A DIFFERENCE IN LIFE.

Obviously, I stayed. I found answers to my questions, reestablished my core values and reaffirmed these values in my life. I rekindled the healing spirit within myself and purposefully found ways to honor and reinforce it daily. I began to manage my emotions, acting on the information they gave me instead of reacting. I wanted to make a difference in life. Where was the need greater than corrections? I would like to say that it was easy from that point on. It wasn't and it still isn't. It was a day-by-day process, a process that you should consider establishing up front.

Let me suggest that you answer those questions for yourself. Confirm and honor your core values, those values for which there is no compromise. Pay attention to your emotions and to what they tell you. Review them daily. Make your decisions using not just your intellect, your reasoning ability, but also your core values and your heart and do not allow anyone to shake you. How will you know if you are on track? One way is to use your family as a barometer, and I will talk to you about that later. First though I want to discuss the third element of my success equation, empathy for other people.

EMPATHY FOR THE OTHER PERSON

At the very heart of success in anything that you endeavor is a *genuine* concern, a *genuine* empathy for the other person. This form of sincere caring is the third element in the success equation. I am not simply speaking of empathy for your coworkers I mean empathy for inmates, for every living person. I learned the importance of empathy over the course of years, but nowhere so well as in parole.

In November 1987, I was promoted to the classification Parole Agent I. As a field agent in San Jose, I carried a very active, downtown caseload. At first, I was a little disconcerted when I went out on my home visits/field calls by myself because I came from the institution where, in case of an incident, back up was only an alarm away. My first solo field call on my own was truly an experience. In the institution I knew exactly what could happen, what harm could befall me, if I was unaware of my surroundings, but I wasn't sure what to expect out in the field.

Gradually, I learned that if I listened, asked the right questions, showed concern and remained sincere in my direction and support, while staying firm but fair in my directives and decisions, I usually avoided conflict and gained support. This experience was reinforced a number of times, but in one case it was particularly obvious.

One man in my caseload had a history of violence. He was about thirty-five, had served several terms for assault with great bodily injury, possession, and a variety of other lesser offenses. He was doing every dime of his parole and was known to not go into custody without a fight when faced with a parole violation. He was not a little man (not that size makes a difference, I have had my butt almost whipped by 4' 10" women); he weighed a solid 220 pounds, every bit of it muscle. His eyes were flat a lot of the time, so was his affect. With his history and propensity for violence, I did not looking forward to his revocation release date.

> WHEN I ASKED WHY HE WENT SO EASILY INTO CUSTODY, HE STATED IT WAS BECAUSE I SEEMED TO CARE, I LISTENED AND WORKED WITH HIM.

I took one look at this guy when he reported for his initial interview and knew beyond a shadow of a doubt that I would never be able to control him physically. I know you are learning about the continuum of force in the Academy; believe me, your capacity for thought, strategy, and empathy is your biggest defense, particularly when you are 5'4" and 125 pounds. I immediately began to develop a relationship with the man.

I talked and listened to him and did everything I could to help him complete a successful parole just as I did every other person on my caseload. Now I am not naïve: I do not think that demonstrating empathy means that you will change old patterns and habits – it won't and it didn't in this man's case. The day came when I had to take him in custody. I did my prearrest planning and took what I thought to be enough back up to safely carry out the arrest. I was surprised; he did not resist. He submitted to my placing him in cuffs without any problems. When I asked why he went so easily into custody, he stated it was because I

seemed to care, I listened and worked with him. He was not the only one who told me that. I cannot begin to count how many times I have had parolees upset at their violations, not because they were in custody, but because they felt they had let me down after I had demonstrated caring or had shown empathy for their situation.

Tony, here is what I learned from over 16 years of similar experiences: not only must you possess the technical skills to perform the functions of your job, you must temper that knowledge with your heart, your principals, values and goals, and have the ability to think in terms of the other person. Keep these skills in balance and use them appropriately.

I have developed an equation to show you what I mean by balance:

Technical Proficiency (TP) + Knowing One's Self (KS) + Empathy of Others (E) = Success

In the scenarios described above, each one of these elements applied at various points. In some situations, success was based solely on my ability to perform the functions of my job, such as planning and effecting a safe arrest, administering medical treatments, and so on. In other scenarios, the pivotal skill involved my ability to make a sound decision or to take an action, appropriate action based on the information I received from my emotions, informed by my principles and values, such as in the shooting incident at Solano. My actions in that incident were not in line with what my heart, my emotions, were telling me, nor with my values and I was miserable, even though my technical skills were excellent. Once I analyzed and corrected my behavior, I was back in balance again and performed much more effectively.

> ... NOT ONLY MUST YOU POSSESS THE TECHNICAL SKILLS ... YOU MUST TEMPER THAT KNOWLEDGE WITH YOUR HEART, YOUR PRINCIPALS, VALUES AND GOALS, AND HAVE THE ABILITY TO THINK IN TERMS OF THE OTHER PERSON.

In the third scenario, I could have done my job, effected the arrest and remained true to my self, without any thought of the person I supervised and I probably could have accomplished my goal of placing the parolee in custody without incident. However, I believe that the parolee's response to my humanity suggests that there was hope for him; he saw something in me that he wanted to emulate. That isn't always the case, which is why you must balance these elements with discretion and observation.

Some inmates and even other staff may initially mistake your use of empathy as a tool for managing relationships for weakness, but they

will soon learn that that isn't the case. It takes even greater discretion and strength to retain you humanity in an environment that does not foster those qualities. In my next letter I will prove to you that there is *power* in compassion and that there will always be persons who respond negatively to such an approach. I am not just talking about your relationship with the inmates but also with your coworkers. Empathy for the other person is an attribute commonly found in the most effective supervisors and managers.

I have heard many people in Corrections say that their supervisors treat them just like inmates. Why? Because, as correctional employees we are taught to command and control. When an individual is rewarded for their job performance with a promotion, they bring those qualities that made them successful in their prior position, command and control. What if we were taught a new way of managing people? What if, at the academy we were taught discretion, the success equation, and our trainers stressed empathy for the other person as well as command and control? Wouldn't that help reduce officer aggression and help them become more effective managers of people?

WHAT IF, AT THE ACADEMY WE WERE TAUGHT DISCRETION, THE SUCCESS EQUATION, AND OUR TRAINERS STRESSED EMPATHY FOR THE OTHER PERSON AS WELL AS COMMAND AND CONTROL?

Balance in all three areas of the success equation is important for another reason. Visualize a tripod. When all three legs function properly, it holds your camera and captures clear, focused pictures of the world. If one of those legs is off balance or missing, you will never achieve clarity, your perception of the world captured in a photo is out of alignment, it's skewed. The same is true of the success equation. A single-minded focus on technical proficiency and knowing yourself leaves you self-absorbed, missing one of life's greatest pleasures, really connecting with the other person. You are off-center, incapable of really establishing relationships that are healthy and enduring. Focusing on the third element, empathy with others, without the balance of intellect or emotional intelligence, can lead to significant pain, such as codependence. These individuals are dangerous in an institution; they often get walked out the door for compromising themselves and the safety of others by thinking only with their heart. They are unable to distinguish the true from the false, and they get caught up in inmate schemes. Such individuals are perpetual victims always acting on skewed perceptions of reality based only on unexplored empathy, untempered by intellect, values, or standards.

How do you achieve balance? I believe that your achieve balance by awareness, education, exploration, and practice. The first step is recognition and awareness that you are a multifaceted person that needs to develop in all the areas of the success equation to create a holistic approach to life. Education, in formal school, in the Academy or self-education all are equally important. A number of books address these issues. I will compile and send you a list of books I have read and found helpful. As you become aware and educate yourself, you need to explore your innermost feelings and actions and measure them against healthy standards, using techniques to strengthen areas that might not be a strong as others. A healthy, successful approach to life can be learned by any person who is motivated enough to try.

Whew! This was a huge letter. We discussed the success equation that I developed over a lifetime of education, experience, and observation. You or anyone can obtain technical proficiency with intelligence and motivation. Knowing yourself includes spiritual grounding, anchoring yourself in your values and goals, understanding the information received from your emotions and using that information appropriately. Having empathy for the other person or being able to think in terms of the other person is also essential. These three principals work like a tripod, all three are required for balance. Try this equation for success, Tony. Consider teaching your children these skills and abilities, as well. It is important that we grow as well-rounded, healthy individuals.

I have given you a lot of food for thought today, and you are probably saying enough is enough. I am going to close for now.

Lots of love,
Mom

> THE FIRST STEP IS RECOGNITION AND AWARENESS THAT YOU ARE A MULTIFACETED PERSON THAT NEEDS TO DEVELOP IN ALL THE AREAS OF THE SUCCESS EQUATION TO CREATE A HOLISTIC APPROACH TO LIFE.

CHAPTER 3

The Power of Compassion

November 5, 1999

Hi Tony,

A ll is well here. I talked to Kim last night; she is taking care of business. She is discovering that she is a strong woman, capable for much more than she gives herself credit. She is blossoming. I want to get over and see the boys this week, but I am not sure when.

How are you adjusting to the military operation at the Training Center? I want to call you by your first name so you will remember it, Muñoz. How are the classes going? Enjoy yourself and learn all you can; you only have this opportunity once. Once you arrive at the institution, you will stay there. Training from that point is all on-site.

Do you feel like you are reading another textbook when you read my letters? I hope not. I am sincerely trying to spare you time, pain and effort by sharing the lessons I've gleaned over 16 years of rich and diverse experience within the department, lessons enriched by stories that reinforce their significance. Speaking of stories, while reading this morning, I remembered another story.

I read an article in *The Futurist*, "Preventing Crime: The Promising Road Ahead," by Gene Stephens, a professor in the College of Criminal Justice, University of South Carolina. He is also editor of *The Police Futurists*. As the former Parole Agent III, Community Correctional Program Manager, my greatest challenge was to develop and implement parolee human service programs that reduced recidivism; so naturally, I was interested in what Stephens had to say. His article discussed the history of crime prevention programs: what works; what doesn't; and what practices show promise, such as community policing and restorative justice. He also comments on the resistance to change within the criminal justice establishment; the resistance to think of their mission as anything other than to rid society of the bad

guys, the parasites. Trust me, getting rid of the parasites is a huge piece of the work, but I believe that task must be balanced by prevention. As Stephens points out, the criminal justice establishment is a huge, multibillion-dollar complex. Many in it are comfortable and secure and are threatened by change. How well I know. Stephen's article reminded me of a story.

In October 1996, the American Correction Association's publication *Corrections Today* honored me as the "Best in the Business" for the success of the Transitional Case Management Program (TCMP). This program, which I developed and implemented, reduced the revocation rate of inmates living with HIV/AIDS and saved taxpayer dollars. According to James Gomez, the Director of Corrections at that time, the TCMP was only the second program in the Department's history to achieve this level of success. The *Corrections Today* article portrayed me as a person who cared, who had compassion for people, which I do. I believe that the success of this program was in part directly related to the caring and compassion of those involved. Tony, there is *power* in compassion. However, not everyone in corrections sees it this way. Let me explain.

CARING OR COMPASSION CAN BE THE KISS OF DEATH IN A DEPARTMENT WHERE THE CULTURE IS PREDICATED ON THE SURVIVAL OF THE FITTEST.

Caring or compassion can be the kiss of death in a department where the culture is predicated on the survival of the fittest. The word "weak" is the worst insult that anyone could hurl at another. Any quality or trait possible to construe as a weakness or vulnerability is suppressed in order to survive. Any quality or trait, which your coworkers believe, would prevent you from carrying out your duties in a less than decisive manner threatens them. In this business, your life and the lives of the inmates in your charge depend on your ability to do your job with strength and courage.

Some people can sense others' vulnerabilities and they manipulate people to the detriment of others. I have seen it happen time and time again. A number of staff has been walked out the door because an inmate or another misguided free person found a weakness and exploited it. But understand this, you can be true to yourself and have concern and respect for humanity, without compromising your decision-making abilities or your integrity. Caring and empathy for the other person is not weak. In fact, I would argue that it takes more strength, coupled with discernment, to have empathy, to care.

Do you remember the story I told you about the day in B1 Clinic when I found that I had become so cold and callous that I didn't recognize myself anymore? That was the day I realized that to regain a healthy balance, I had to reacquaint myself with my core concepts and values and to honor and commit to living by those values. Over the years I have stayed true to that decision. It hasn't always been easy.

After the "Best in the Business" article was released, I received several comments from coworkers regarding "my social work traits." I received very little positive feedback. You must understand that this article was released just as the Corcoran incidents, in which the officers were alleged to have staged gladiator-style fights, came to light and the Department was received terrible press. It needed a positive spin. Somewhat dismayed with the negative comments, I spoke to my administrator who concurred with my position that it takes courage to live by values, to retain feelings when so many around you grow numb or become so brutalized they lose their ability to care. Tony, caring isn't weak, there is power in compassion, and it has been proven. Respect for humanity, honoring, and living by your values isn't weak. It takes resolve and discernment. But in the end, you go home with yourself at night. In the final analysis, you will be judged by your strength of character, not by the compromises that you make to fit in.

YOU MUST DO SOMETHING TO COUNTERACT THE NEGATIVITY YOU ENCOUNTER EVERY DAY IN THE WORKPLACE.

So, how do you maintain your balance? You must do something to counteract the negativity you encounter every day in the workplace. You must find a way to give back to the community. Engage in an activity that comes from your heart. You have two sons, stay involved in their lives, coach their sports teams, mentor them and any disadvantaged children you meet along the way. This is nothing new for you; you have always been involved with your kids because you love them. Now, that involvement is critical for your own well-being and that of your family. You must feed your heart with the same consistency with which you are confronted with negativity at work.

Other suggestions for feeding your heart:

• **Volunteer with Big Brothers/Big Sisters;**

• **Join a mentoring programs for disadvantaged youth;**

• **Assist the elderly with such activities of life as lawn care, shopping, rides to medical appointments;**

• **Go to the schools and speak to children about drugs;**

- **Teach reading through a library literacy program;**

- **Donate food and clothing to help the poor; or**

- **Volunteer at church.**

I continued to work as a nurse in the community, between the nursing and being a mother, I reinforced my caring nature, I fed my heart. There are a variety of ways in which you can give back to the community and meet good people who lead healthy, happy lives, a barometer by which you can gauge yourself. Volunteering and giving back restores your faith in humanity; it counteracts the poison of evil and the negativity of the workplace. It helps reinforce those standards and principals that are important: caring for and serving others and giving of yourself.

VOLUNTEERING AND GIVING BACK RESTORES YOUR FAITH IN HUMANITY; IT COUNTERACTS THE POISON OF EVIL AND THE NEGATIVITY OF THE WORKPLACE.

If you truly want to be a good correctional officer, an officer who makes a difference, do your job with all the skills and abilities you possess, yet realize that is only one third of the equation. The other parts of the equation involve anchoring yourself in your standards, values, and goals and caring for the other person. Reinforce those values in the work you do for the community; after all, the ultimate crime abatement program is prevention.

Think about these things, Tony. There is power in compassion. Caring takes courage, conviction, and reinforcement. Giving of your self to others by volunteering in the community is one way to accomplish that reinforcement. Feed your heart with as much ambition as you place in your career, and you will come out the winner. I love you and want only the best for you and your family.

Love,
Mom

Discerning Follower-ship™

November 10, 1999

Hi There,

Week two, and I am so glad that you are enjoying yourself, have found instructors you respect, and are doing well academically. What is the news here, you ask? You are so close and yet so far away. First of all, I think I have your Grandma talked into going to Mexico with us over Thanksgiving week. Your aunt Deanna is having a hard time pulling it together, so I am going to find out if I can change the name on her ticket. Mom is very excited about that.

The other news is about your cousin, Sean. He had some health problems, went to the doctor, and they found cancer cells in his urine. They performed a MRI that almost killed him because he was allergic to the dye, but they removed a cancer from his bladder. When they repeated the tests, though they found more cancer cells. They are now looking at his kidney. I emailed him and asked him to let me know what the results were. I will let you know when I hear.

I spoke with Kim last night, and all is well over there. We plan to go to Apple Hill and Christmas shopping. Anthony wants a telescope for Christmas. I am going to ask his teacher what they studied that stimulated his interest and then find him a gift that will build on that enthusiasm. I don't know what I will get Devante, I am sure he will tell me exactly what he wants.

I read in the paper last night that the officers from Corcoran were acquitted of charges in the "booty bandit" rape case. I am sure that they are relieved that the trial is over and that the officers were absolved of any wrongdoing. The trial brought back many memories of my experiences in the institutions, rare (more rare than some would like to think) situations in which someone had to decide

between choosing to protect a coworker by silence or to speak out and rectify a wrong. I remember one night in particular.

The site was B1 Clinic (I told you about all the action that occurred there), nightshift, and I was on duty. The Medical Officer of the Day (MOD) was about twenty minutes away in a house on institution property. I rarely got frivolous calls at night. If the phone rang, it was usually an emergency. That particular night, I got a "man-down" call from an officer on Q-wing, a psychiatric housing unit. I responded with a gurney and found the man had slashed his wrists and claimed to have eaten razor blades. Fortunately, he had missed any major arteries, and we transported him safely back to the clinic for treatment.

The protocol in those days was to notify the MOD that he/she was needed in the clinic, give a report on the situation, and then follow the doctor's orders until

INSTEAD OF FOLLOWING THE **MOD**'S ORDERS, I CHOOSE TO LISTEN TO MY VOICE OF CONSCIENCE IN A VERY DIFFICULT SITUATION.

arrival. That particular night, the doctor sounded a bit strange, in fact downright drunk. I ordered x-rays and began setting up a sterile field so the doctor could suture the wounds. The doctor arrived so drunk he walked sideways, completely unable to perform his duties. In slurred words, he told me that the son-of-a-bitch was faking and to send him back to the unit. I could not believe my eyes or ears.

I knew from rumors that he liked his sauce and that this kind of thing had happened before, but this was the first time I had experienced the situation. The Watch Commander that night was a good man; in fact, I have worked with him often over the years. That night was the first time I had ever worked with him, yet he supported me in my actions when I defied the doctor's orders and had the man sent out to the local community hospital for treatment. The incident was reported and the doctor, although he remained on staff, was not allowed to serve as a MOD again. I do not know if he was referred to treatment or if any other administrative sanctions were applied.

What is my point? Instead of following the MOD's orders, I choose to listen to my voice of conscience in a very difficult situation. The Watch Commander supported my actions. He refused to sweep the incident under the rug. He knew the doctor was a "good old boy" and he knew that this incident had happened before, without anyone taking action. We stood our ground; the doctor was not allowed to serve as MOD for a period of time, which probably saved many a person, including staff, as he would have been on call if they were hurt also.

Whatever your position, I've learned that some times you need to lead, other times you need to follow. You will play both roles in life. Life is full of choices, and the path that you follow is determined by the essence of your character. While a wealth of information exists on leadership, not much has been written about follower-ship, yet this idea is so important, I've given it a name "Discerning Follower-ship™." Discerning follower-ship is the ability to perceive or recognize that something is different than the norm, measuring that difference against the yardstick of right values and principals, and then consciously making a decision whether to follow or resist. Sounds simple, but in many situations, it's difficult to practice. Let me explain.

Hannah Arendt's book *Eichman in Jerusalem: A Report on the Banality of Evil,* which I plan to discuss in a future letter, speaks to people in Nazi Germany who were inwardly opposed to the Holocaust but who chose to say nothing and so the slaughter continued. The book further discloses that in cases where people resisted based on principal, many lives were saved. Jerry B. Harvey's *The Abilene Paradox* explains that our need for connection with others and our fear that we will be separated from that support frames the dynamics that lead to collusion with evil or with actions in contradiction to what we know to be right. Successful discerning followers must develop and trust in their intuition.

FACED WITH AN INSTANT DECISION THAT MAY OR MAY NOT RING TRUE, MANY ARE HESITANT TO LISTEN TO THE GUIDANCE OF THEIR INNER VOICE.

Our culture is so focused on the scientific method of solving problems, using logic and reason, that intuition has been scorned as an emotional response attributed unbecomingly to women. Faced with an instant decision that may or may not ring true, many are hesitant to listen to the guidance of their inner voice. Trusting only in mountains of facts, logic, and reason, eliminates a major piece of intelligence, emotions.

A growing number of studies are demonstrating that emotions, gut level responses, are often more accurate than logic in sound decision making. Emotions complete the intelligence component of the success equation. Learning to trust and respond to your inner voice, your intuition, is essential. Because we have been taught all of our lives that emotions have no place in a decision, we allow ourselves to be placed in situations that may compromise our integrity. Challenging others we assume know more than we do, who have greater authority than ourselves, or in a group of peers where there is no other dissenting voice, can be difficult but can lead to the best outcomes.

For example, people who work in Corrections tend to form cliques and to be accepted in those cliques; a person must conform to their code of behavior. Challenging those group norms can be difficult. Why?

Because of the underlying message, you are either for us or against us and, if you challenge us, you will be blackballed. This is an intimidating message in an environment where you must rely on your peers for your survival. Here is only one example.

One day about three weeks into my career, I was working in B1 Clinic, when several male officers brought in an inmate who had been in an altercation. I need to paint you a picture of the clinic in those days. There was not a lot of control. When the inmates were released for chow, they were allowed to come into the clinic for "hot meds," or controlled medications, to sign up for sick call or for any other medical emergency that might occur. This was the institution nerve center for medical care. It was very hectic.

In any event, I examined the inmate, documented my observations, and planned interventions when a candid, no-holds-barred conversation broke out about anal intercourse and how the inmates had to fight to protect their "booties." The conversation was rough, vulgar and, quite frankly, embarrassing. I was not sure how to respond since my views were obviously out of step with the rest. Now this wasn't a conversation that just the inmates were having; the officers were involved as well. Someone finally spoke up and said, "We don't need to be talking like this; there is a lady present." It got deathly quiet in the clinic. For what seemed like an eternity, all eyes were upon me waiting for my response to the comment. Then the officers informed me that I knew where I was working and I would just have to get used to it.

I am sorry to say that in my quest for acceptance, I did get used to it. Not only did I get used to it; I became quite capable of throwing out a few zingers myself. I would like to say that I was a trailblazer, that I stood my ground and fought for my rights, but I did not. I did not know that I had any rights. I succumbed to the pressure, to the message that in order to survive, I had to adjust because the system would not adjust for me. It was not easy.

A new person from the Academy, malleable and wanting to make a good impression, is in a difficult position. Expecting that the experienced officers are professional, wanting to be accepted, new staff are

> I WOULD LIKE TO SAY
> THAT I WAS A
> TRAILBLAZER, THAT
> I STOOD MY GROUND
> AND FOUGHT FOR MY
> RIGHTS, BUT I DID NOT.
> I DID NOT KNOW THAT
> I HAD ANY RIGHTS.

liable to swallow their concerns and ignore their inner voice when faced with the statement: "This is the way we have always done things." Soon the new person is part and parcel of the system, a chain that is difficult to break without intervention. We need to give people permission to trust their intuition, to stand for what they know to be true, if the system is to improve.

Harvey opens *The Abilene Paradox* by describing four adults who take a miserable journey through a hot dessert and eat terrible food in a place no one wanted to go. I love this book! The author took a humorous look at managing agreement and applied it to the corporate setting. He describes the destruction that can occur if no one is willing to stand their ground and speak up for what they know to be true. The same destruction occurs in the correctional environment when people are afraid to speak their convictions. Harvey goes further when he explains that speaking up is actually the best service we can provide to our employers/others. He then explores the reasons for our willingness not to speak up. It takes courage and the resolve to fight fiercely to maintain the right values and to stand by them when working in the correctional environment.

WHAT DO YOU DO IN A SITUATION IN WHICH YOU ARE THE FOLLOWER, WHEN THE PERSON IN CHARGE IS DOING SOMETHING YOU KNOW IS WRONG?

What do you do in a situation in which you are the follower, when the person in charge is doing something you know is wrong? What do you do when your partner got out of line and you feel the tremendous peer pressure to keep your mouth shut? You can be sure that if you observe improprieties, others are also aware of them.

You walk a tightrope, Tony. If you choose to stay healthy, if you want to be a discerning follower, consider developing the following characteristics. A discerning follower is:

- **Intuitive:** Discerning followers understand, trust, and are not afraid to act on their inner voice.

- **Courageous:** Discerning followers have their own definition of courage. Anchored in the right values and principals, they know that true courage involves standing their ground in opposition to what they know to be wrong, and they are not afraid to fight fiercely.

- **Discerning:** With the ability to separate one thing mentally from another or others.

- **Bi-directional:** Having the confidence and ability to lead or follow; able to fill in a vacuum.

- **Solid:** Anchored in the right values with the ability to measure actions against the yardstick of solid principals.

- **Non-assuming:** Discerning followers do not assume that others will automatically do the right thing in spite of position, authority, or influence.

- **Independent thinkers:** Not swayed by rank, position, authority, or groupthink.

I am not suggesting that you refuse to follow orders because that is a must in Corrections. I am suggesting that in addition to developing the aforementioned characteristics that you consider the following.

IF YOUR GUT TELLS YOU THAT SOMETHING ISN'T RIGHT, LISTEN AND RESPECT IT. AND DO NOT BECOME COMPLACENT; COMPLACENCY IS THE BIGGEST ENEMY OF ALL.

- **Practice prevention:** Position yourself up front as a man who is principle driven, who has convictions from which he will not bend. This will go a long way to prevent behavioral indiscretions by misguided staff or inmates while you are on watch. Do not bend the first time because after that it gets easier.

- **Rely on policy and procedure:** If a coworker or a supervisor suggests an inappropriate action, gently ask that person to pardon your ignorance, that this action is not part of any policy or procedure of which you are aware.

- **Make your position clear:** If an incident does occur, let your coworkers know that you don't play that way and that you will report any further transgressions to the supervisor. Report them if they reoccur. Trust me, the information that you are a man of principle will spread, quicker than you can imagine.

- **Document, document, and document!**

People who bend the rules in one situation will do so in another. Learn who you can rely on and learn to avoid – where possible – those who cut corners. Tony, learn to trust yourself. Listen more than you talk. Think, and ask yourself what motives drive such action. Be constantly aware and hone your intuition. If your gut tells you that something isn't right, listen and respect it. And do not become complacent; complacency is the biggest enemy of all.

We, as a people, need to learn to be discerning followers. People are so desperate for social acceptance, guidance, and leadership they will just about follow anyone. Take a look at history: Hitler; Jim Jones; even Charlie Manson. Manson was not the least mesmerizing to me when I worked with him in the institution, but to followers he was. He used cult development techniques successfully (check out the Internet, he still has a following after 30 years). Look at those people who followed Marshal Applewhite, who led his followers to their death in a mass suicide attempting to catch the Hale-Bopp comet (Applewhite's nickname was "Do," which should have given potential followers a clue). Finally, following has a bad name; it doesn't mean you stop thinking for yourself.

I have covered a lot of ground in this letter. We talked about the importance of being a discerning follower and the dire consequences of not doing so. We reviewed the qualities that are important and discussed ways to position yourself in the institution to prevent problems from following misdirected staff. Think well on these things before you start working and you will find yourself much better able to manage the complexities of the job.

Well, enough for today. I look forward to talking to you this weekend. Your experiences are really taking me back. I loved my career in Corrections. Some folks do not understand that. They would rather work in what they perceive to be a safer environment. Sometimes I have to laugh at people outside of the correctional system. We know what to expect from the inmates and can be prepared. Those of whom we have no expectations can harm us most easily (look at the workplace shootings). See you this weekend.

Lots of Love,
Mom

I LOVED MY CAREER IN CORRECTIONS. SOME FOLKS DO NOT UNDERSTAND THAT.

CHAPTER 5

Eichman in the Institution or The Face of Evil

November 13, 1999

Dear Tony:

H ow are you? We miss you! It seems funny to have you away and not at least phone accessible. In any event, life goes on and you will be home before we know it.

Last night on television news two men were being arraigned for several murders, one of which occurred over fourteen years ago. The parents of that girl had the most interesting comment. During the course of the investigation, and as time passed without finding the perpetrator, they had built an image of the person who had committed the crimes as a monster. When they saw the pair that the courts accused of committing the crime, they exclaimed that the accused were "just people." I understand. One of the first things I noticed when working in corrections was that men who looked like my baby brother and the youth pastor had committed the most heinous crimes. To use an old, hackneyed saying "You can't always judge a book by its cover."

I am not speaking about those folks who are fairly obvious. To this day when I walk down the street and see a person covered with jail-house tattoos, I wonder whose caseload they are on and tend to stay away from them. Folks who are obviously mentally unbalanced or those in a road rage are equally obvious. No, I am talking about those who look innocuous, are articulate, have a logical message, and sometimes work in positions of authority. I am not talking just of inmates, but fellow staff and free people within the community.

Why is this letter necessary? Unfortunately, in this life you will be exposed to individuals who are evil, who lack moral boundaries and, given the position of discretionary power, who will abuse that power. Fortunately, such individuals are rare, but you will meet or even work with someone like this at least once in your career. Some of them you can easily recognize because it appears as if the main purpose of their day is to agitate inmates and to create scenarios that result in physical escalation. But there are other subtler behaviors which demand your attention. The majority of the people you work with will be decent law-abiding citizens who try to make a better life for themselves and their families. Men and women, much like yourself, who go to work and just want the day to flow without problems or difficulties, who enforce the regulations fairly and firmly. It is for both of these groups that I write this letter. This letter is necessary because you need the tools to recognize and guard yourself against the actions of those who would abuse their power. You need to avoid inadvertently getting caught up in a scenario that is injurious to yourself or others, so that you and the others can go home at night safely and in good conscience. You cannot always know what to expect from a person just from the way they look.

... YOU NEED THE TOOLS TO RECOGNIZE AND GUARD YOURSELF AGAINST THE ACTIONS OF THOSE WHO WOULD ABUSE THEIR POWER.

This fact is corroborated in Hannah Arendt's *Eichman in Jerusalem: A Report on the Banality of Evil.* I am sure you remember from your history classes that Adolf Eichman, a Nazi leader, was responsible for the transportation of the Jews and other "undesirables" to the death camps during World War II. He was a common man, of average intelligence and looks, whom a number of psychiatrists during the course of his trial for war crimes, certified as "normal." He did not hate the Jews, and he was not a fanatic nor cynical but nonetheless, Eichman helped effect the murder of millions of individuals. He was not alone. Doctors, lawyers, bankers, business leaders, fine, upstanding pillars of the community, sat on many committees tasked with the responsibility of managing the "Jewish problem." What happened? Why do people we assume to live by a set of morals and principals participate in activities like the Holocaust? What lessons are there in this event for us? What lessons are there for Corrections?

When I read this book I was chilled by the descriptions of Nazi culture and it's similarity to some aspects of the prison culture. I want to be careful here. Please be clear, I am not saying that Corrections is a Nazi organization. I am saying that some of the behaviors observed early in the Nazi's rise to power, which eventually led to the death of over 12,000,000 people, are evident in Corrections. This similarity should raise some red flags. Let me explain.

DISCRIMINATION

The people involved in the prison camp atrocities did not just wake up one day and start slaughtering others. The holocaust started very simply, with discrimination against the Jews and other "inferiors," mentally ill, union members, gays, disabled people, etc. They were not allowed to take civil service jobs, a small assault against principles, not a major transgression, so it was easy enough to ignore. Of course, we know what happened as a result of the ever-larger and more damaging incursions on individual rights in Nazi Germany. The underlying attitude expressed by so many "average" people in Nazi Germany was one of complacency, of acceptance of the institutionally defined "us versus them," rather than a general intent to enslave and kill entire groups of people.

This underlying attitude is not really so different from the "us versus them" attitude held by so many in Corrections. "They" are the criminals and "we" are the "good" people. How can we tell? Because "they" are behind bars, while "we" remain free. It's a harmless and rather just idea at first glance. Right? But, when you take a deeper look, you realize that this very attitude perpetuates much of the distress so prevalent in the Correctional System today. It is discrimination on everyone's part, the inmates and free staff, and must be addressed if the system is to remain healthy. So how do we address this attitude? It starts with one truthful person.

"THEY" ARE THE CRIMINALS AND "WE" ARE THE "GOOD" PEOPLE. HOW CAN WE TELL?

Does not the law, as Arendt states in her book, "presuppose precisely that we have a common humanity with those whom we accuse and judge and condemn?" Further, isn't one of the most important actions we can take for another human being is to hold them accountable for their actions? I believe that accountability is a simple solution for a complicated problem. It moves us out of the realm of the "us versus them" and begins to set the stage for a greater respect for humanity, which is essential to combat the insidious effects of evil.

NORMAL

We consider ourselves "normal," impervious to the insidious onslaughts against our principals and values. The "us versus them" attitude further aids us in the self-deception that we are somehow different than the criminal we supervise. We believe that their misfortunes were the result of a clear choice made by a morally bankrupt

individual, and that we are somehow immune to the frailties and weaknesses of the human spirit. This belief is a mistake and makes us vulnerable to the same deceptions that allowed the "normal" people in Nazi Germany and Eastern Europe to become involved in an abhorrent event that flies in the face of human decency, principles, and morals.

There are a variety of reasons that these "normal" people might have cooperated; they seem obvious in hindsight. One of those reasons was that the Nazis had a language rule. They would rely on euphemisms; for example, the "final solution" so they would not have to use words like murder or exterminate, killing by gas and other tortures, was covered under the euphemism "medical matters." They glossed over what they were actually doing. What does this have to do with corrections? On occasion, I have heard coworkers use euphemisms for misconduct. For example, a Corrections Officer stated that an inmate had received some "thumb therapy" for some transgression they had committed or a "housing change" when an inmate refused to cooperate in an investigation or some other transgression and was placed in a cell in a situation where the inmate would very likely get hurt. Both are euphemisms for what was actually officer aggression and violence.

> ACCEPTING OR SUPPORTING ANY ACTION THAT DOES NOT "RING TRUE" WITH YOUR VALUES SETS THE STAGE FOR EVEN FURTHER COMPROMISE WITH EVIL.

Accepting or supporting any action that does not "ring true" with your values sets the stage for even further compromise with evil. Tony, truth is tremendously important; acknowledging human vulnerabilities up front goes a long way toward protecting us from egregious assaults on our conscience.

HUMANITY AS A WEAKNESS

Human emotions were not tolerated in the Nazi regime; emotions were seen as a deterrent to getting the job done. Nor is caring and humanity an attribute favored in the institution. It is seen as weak, not by all but by many. I have already written you a letter, detailing my experiences, and the power I found in compassion. Tony, I can only emphasize it again that caring and concern for humanity is not weak. It actually takes more strength to care. Can you imagine what would have happened if one of those normal people would have voiced some concern, would have resisted on principle. The Germans would not have succeeded and it happened in some areas.

The Germans could not do what they did on their own. They needed assistance, and they received it from many arenas, including from the victims. Without the help of the Jewish Councils and police they could not have accomplished what they did. When they met resistance, they failed. The Danes resisted, and many of the Jews in Denmark were saved. Tony, you do not know what the power of a stand on principle will accomplish. I am sure that those who stood by their principles in the face of extreme danger did not know as well, but they acted consciously and were able to save the lives of thousands of people. Remember that lesson. Respect your humanity and the humanity in others. Do let evil gain a foothold because once it does it is more difficult to diminish.

LACK OF EMPATHY

What struck me as I read Arendt's book was that Eichman was described as lacking in empathy for the other person. He was unable to think from the standpoint of others. Nowhere is the lack of empathy for the other person and its results more profound than in the example of the Holocaust. More recent examples are far too commonplace: Bosnia, Serbia, in the killing fields of Laos, the gassing of Turks in Iraq, or in those countries where the militants go into villages and systematically amputate an arm or a leg of each villager (some allow victims to "choose" which appendage they wish to lose). Are not our inner cities, our schools, or the workplace, where aggression is becoming an increasing method of handling disputes, examples of our inability to empathize with the other person? As I wrote in my formula for success, we must learn empathy for the other person in order to succeed in our personal lives, in our communities, in our governments, and in our nations.

RESPECT YOUR HUMANITY AND THE HUMANITY IN OTHERS. DO LET EVIL GAIN A FOOTHOLD BECAUSE ONCE IT DOES IT IS MORE DIFFICULT TO DIMINISH.

Evil does not always manifest itself in deceitful ways; sometimes the evil is blatant, in your face, and can affect your health physically and mentally. It happened to me when I was promoted to the classification Parole Agent III, managing the Parole and Community Services Division's Sexually Violent Predator Program. I was tasked with oversight of the review of the case of any parolee in the revocation process, whose commitment offense met the criteria set forth in law, specifically persons who had committed certain sex offenses. Individuals whose convictions met these criteria were forwarded to the District Attorney of the committing county.

The District Attorney would then determine if they would take the case forward for a possible civil commitment in Atascadero State Hospital for treatment after they had served their prison time.

It was my job to review the cases forwarded to Central Office to determine if they should move forward in the process. Tony, I did not want to know the things I learned about the capacity for evil that people seem to embody, nor about the acts they can perpetuate upon one another; it was so far outside of my previous experience. After all, most of the prison population is made up of property and drug offenders. Reviewing the cases submitted for inclusion in the Sexually Violent Predator program, I was confronted with crimes so horrible I could not comprehend them. I did not realize people were capable of such brutality. Page after page of gruesome crimes: mutilations, torture, murder, rape, bestiality and worst of all, people who did not just molest children but tortured them sexually, pedophiles in the worst sense.

I DID NOT TRUST ANYONE. I KEPT MY DOORS BOLTED AND SLEPT WITH MY WEAPON HANDY. NO ONE WAS GOING TO RAPE OR TORTURE ME.

Day after day, week after week, I was immersed in this poison. What do you do with your feelings when you go home? There are no lockers in which you can store your brain until you return the next day. It made me sick; literally. My poor husband – if I fell asleep before him, when he tried to come to bed; I woke up startled and tried to take him out, thinking that he was an intruder. I dreamed nightly of people coming through my windows trying to mutilate me. I did not trust anyone. I kept my doors bolted and slept with my weapon handy. No one was going to rape or torture me.

Where does a person go for help with such feelings? Did others feel as I did? If so, they didn't acknowledge it to me. They went about their business as if the content of our work was commonplace. I went to Sex Offender Conferences, hoping the presenters could shed some light on the subject and learned a tremendous amount, mostly taught through case studies of the worst offenders. While I acquired state-of-the-art knowledge, I felt sick from the examples training used, and I was still unable to manage the stress of the position. Denial didn't work. I put on the "I can handle anything" face but it did not work either. I carried that stress the whole year I was assigned to that program. Denial gets you nowhere that you really want to go. Right after that assignment I had my heart attack.

I started this letter talking about how the holocaust started with simple discrimination and that the eventual murder of millions of individuals rested partly in the hands of "normal" people who were unable to empathize with others and who believed that any display of emotions or humanity is a weakness. We know that some of those same behaviors can be observed in the correctional environment. We know that evil manifests itself in many deceitful and compelling ways and that compromise leads to complacency. Other times evil is blatant and in your face, and you must deal with it. Regardless of how it presents itself, the effects on our mind, body, and spirit are much the same. It is injurious and contributes greatly to the stress of the system. What is the remedy to evil? What can we do to protect ourselves, to make us less vulnerable to its taint?

Tony, when you work in an institution, you are out of the public's view. Isolation is dangerous; it creates breeding grounds for distortions of what is acceptable. The isolated culture creates its own meaning and, when acclimating to a new, isolated environment, a person can very easily be mislead and compromised. It is difficult to go into a new environment such as corrections, without wanting desperately to blend in, to be accepted, to show that you are capable of handling anything thrown at you, a "hog." It is easy to become accepting of behaviors that most healthy people would question, especially when everyone around you accepts abnormal behavior as "normal." At just this point, you must hold on to your standards and values, and not become a man of compromise. The first time that a fellow officer or a superior suggests "some thumb therapy" for an errant inmate, or the first time that an inmate suggests a compromising behavior, you must stand your ground. Believe me, in the long run, your word, your standards, and your refusal to compromise will make your reputation and garner much more respect. In the final analysis, you must go home with yourself – every night.

IT IS EASY TO BECOME ACCEPTING OF BEHAVIORS THAT MOST HEALTHY PEOPLE WOULD QUESTION, ESPECIALLY WHEN EVERYONE AROUND YOU ACCEPTS ABNORMAL BEHAVIOR AS "NORMAL."

Here are some suggestions:

- **Sunshine your behavior, for one.** Do not do anything that you would present to the state legislature or to the media because that is exactly where you will go if you get caught.

- **Be aware, not paranoid.** Question the motives of those around you, live by your intuition, and measure your decisions and behavior by the yardstick of principles, values, and morals.

- **Stand your ground and live by the standards that you know to be true.** Resist anything that falls short of those standards.

- **Discuss issues of concern with others.** You can be sure that if you are questioning the appropriateness of an action, so are others.

- **Retain and respect the humanity in yourself as well as in others.** Be accountable for your behavior and hold others accountable for theirs.

- **Be aware and beware of the "us versus them" attitude which prevails in the institution.** How does it contribute to the environment? Is it healthy? What can you do to overcome the barriers that this attitude erects?

... RECONFIRM YOUR IDENTITY AND GOALS, AND BECOME A WISE MAN WHO CAN LOOK BACK ON LIFE AND FEEL GLAD THAT YOU DID A JOB WELL DONE AND THAT YOU STOOD FOR SOMETHING ALL YOUR DAYS.

- **In terms of health maintenance, take care of your mind as well as you take care of your body in preparation for the physical demands of your job.** Limit your exposure to evil and promote healthy, nurturing situations to counteract its impact.

- **Obtain the assistance of a professional counselor when necessary.** You will encounter actions and behaviors in the institution that are difficult to digest and they will impact your life. California Department of Corrections has an Employee Assistance Program that will pay for counseling in some situations. Take advantage of that.

- **Manage stress by taking care of your body with a healthy diet, exercise, and consistent training.**

Tony, do you just want to unlock gates and give the inmates what they have coming or do you want to be an officer who shines like a beacon of light, a positive example. Do you want to collect a check or make a difference in the lives of those around you? Are you a leader of principle, willing to stand your ground? Make that determination right now, reconfirm your identity and goals, and become a wise man who can look back on life and feel glad that you did a job well done and that you stood for something all your days.

Lots of Love,
Mom

CHAPTER 6

Intuition and Fear, Healthy Attributes

November 19, 1999

Hi!

How are you, Tony? Plugging right along as usual? I am going to Woodland this morning to videotape the storyteller I gifted to your son's class. She will tell stories for about forty minutes and then answer questions. I went to Costco and bought some snacks for the kids and am bringing the video camera to capture the moment. I will probably enjoy this as much as the kids do. It is truly the little things in life that make it worth living. I so enjoy my grandkids; visiting them allows me to forget the cares of life for a moment.

What fun it was to see you Sunday night and to meet your friends. You are so excited about what you are doing, learning all you can about your new career. It speaks to the excellent job that your instructors are doing at the Academy. Your enthusiasm is infectious. I was ready to count cadence and go to the range. If you had any misgivings, it certainly didn't show, and that is my concern. I see a lot of bravado and "We are tough; we can do it attitude," but without any expression of legitimate concerns or fears. The "fear of showing weakness" mindset is so common in Corrections but is so injurious. The correctional culture has already begun to grow on you.

Fear is a normal, healthy response. If I were not at least a little bit intimidated about working in a prison, which is fraught with danger, I would be concerned. Fear is nature's alarm; it protects you from danger. Let me explain.

The dictionary defines fear as a feeling of anxiety and agitation caused by the presence of or nearness of danger, evil or pain, as a feeling of uneasiness or apprehension. Sometimes we cannot initially explain why we are frightened or alarmed. We know intuitively that something is amiss and, instead of honoring that instinct without crit-

icism or censure, we deny our truest, most basic ability to protect ourselves, intuition. Intuition is the direct knowing or learning of something without conscious reasoning, immediate apprehension, or understanding. Intuition and fear work hand in hand.

It is generally accepted that early, prehistoric people depended on the 5 physical senses for survival, sight, smell, hearing, taste, touch; and the sixth sense, intuition. These six senses were each honed to perfection. As people developed tools to ease existence and problem solving became more of an exercise in the scientific theory and reductionism reasoning, the less the senses were honored. Intuition, over the years, became diluted by judgement and denial, filtered through a lens of reason and attributed unbecomingly to the emotions of women. As man questioned and then began to deny his/her intuition, he/she became less effective in business dealings and relationships with other people.

INTUITION, OVER THE YEARS, BECAME DILUTED BY JUDGEMENT AND DENIAL, FILTERED THROUGH A LENS OF REASON AND ATTRIBUTED UNBECOMINGLY TO THE EMOTIONS OF WOMEN.

It is only in recent years, when success in business and life demands faster and smarter answers and when competition in the global economy has accelerated the pace of business, that we had to explore other means of knowing. There has been a resurgence of interest in the part that emotional intelligence, including intuition, has in making decisions, developing effective relationships, and intelligence. We are now confirming what the earliest people knew, that intuition and emotional intelligence is the springboard to successful living.

This is not a new revelation to me. Intuition and healthy fear have been my best friends for years. As a field Parole Agent in Santa Clara County, I supervised a caseload of felons and civil addicts. When a parolee was released, we completed a risk and needs assessment that assigned a score, which designated the level of supervision the individual warranted. The level of supervision dictated the minimum amount of contact we were to have during a specific time frame. Making field contacts at the person's home or place of employment, assessing their environment and lifestyle, and making judgements about the observations were essential components of supervision. You learned more about a person in one field visit than you ever could sitting behind the desk conducting an interview. We worked by ourselves in the field and went into the homes of very dangerous felons without the backup I had become accustomed to in the institution. Safety is paramount and depends upon the agent's ability to use their six senses, much as did prehistoric man.

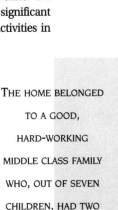

I remember one hot July day, 98 degrees, unusual for San Jose. I was out in the field early, trying to beat the heat. I had a number of home visits I wanted to accomplish that morning, eight in all. I had an appointment with one of my parolees whom I needed to arrest that afternoon in the office and a report to write for the Board of Prison Terms before the day was over for an arrest that I had made two days prior. I had an active, downtown caseload, which kept me moving.

The first six home visits went as expected. I contacted either the parolee or I was able to make a collateral (spouse, family, or significant other) contact and received some great information on activities in which my parolees had been involved, which warranted future interventions on my part. I arrived at the 7th house, somewhat concerned about what I would find, but not overly anxious.

The home belonged to a good, hard-working middle-class family who, out of seven children, had two with major psychiatric and drug problems, both on my caseload. The eldest of the two was in custody. The San Jose Police Department arrested him for being under the influence of PCP and resisting arrest. When I went to the jail to interview him, he showed me bruises he'd received from the batons used during the arrest incident. It appeared as if there had been a major battle, the parolee the loser. I always marvel at the mindset of these individuals. They do everything they can to injure or kill the arresting officers and then get angry because the police had to use the force necessary to take them into custody. He said and I quote: "I know I was wrong, but they didn't have to do this." "Well, what would you have them do?" I responded, "let you hurt them?" The point I am trying to make is that both brothers had the potential for violence.

THE HOME BELONGED TO A GOOD, HARD-WORKING MIDDLE CLASS FAMILY WHO, OUT OF SEVEN CHILDREN, HAD TWO WITH MAJOR PSYCHIATRIC AND DRUG PROBLEMS, BOTH ON MY CASELOAD.

The second brother had not appeared for his scheduled appointment several weeks before, and I needed to contact him to find out what was going on in his life. Although his arrest history indicated Control Supervision, the potential for violence warranted closer supervision because of concern for his level of dangerousness. I visited his house several times after he had missed his appointment and the family told me that he was not at home. I left a message for him to contact me, but he had not responded. This was my third attempt to contact him, which if unsuccessful would force me to place a Parolee at Large warrant in the system.

I pulled up to the ranch style house, which looked like it held a healthy, happy intact family, without any major problems. The lawn was landscaped and well maintained. The house was freshly painted, beautifully furnished, and very clean. Two cars were parked outside, an older BMW and an SUV. This was a traditional family, in which Mother stayed home and served as caretaker while Father was the earner and undisputed head of the family. When their sons were paroled, the family was oriented to the conditions of parole and told how having a parolee living within their house would impact their privacy. They were educated about conditions of parole including parole searches and agreed that the sons could continue to live in their home. I must say, Tony, because of your brother, I understand how a troubled family member can tear a family asunder. Hope and conflicting loyalties constantly divide you. You are challenged to support troubled family members who are not always truthful, yet bound by the need to be respectful of their conditions of parole. It is not an enviable position, and such was the case with this family.

ALL APPEARED AS IT HAD BEEN EVERY OTHER TIME I HAD VISITED THIS HOME, BUT MY GUT TOLD ME THAT SOMETHING WAS DIFFERENT, THAT SOMETHING DID NOT ADD UP.

I approached the house noting nothing out of the ordinary and knocked at the door, which was answered by the mother. She proceeded to tell me that her son was not home, that he still lived there, and that she had given him my messages. All appeared as it had been every other time I had visited this home, but my gut told me that something was different, that something did not add up. I looked briefly around the house and did not find anything amiss, so I left another message with the mother and continued about my day. After I completed my final house call, I had a feeling that if I went back and did a thorough parole search with backup that I would find my missing parolee.

I did just that. I went to the office, spoke to my supervisor, and got another agent. In addition, I called for a uniformed backup from San Jose Police Department. Back at the residence I found my parolee, blasted on PCP, and it took everybody we had to get him in custody. He was a slight man, 5'8" and 145 pounds, yet he fought like a tiger. The other agent, concerned that calling in uniformed backup was like confessing that we couldn't manage our parolees, was grateful for the support.

After the fact, the mother told me that he came home that morning under the influence. He terrorized her for several hours before settling down, just before my arrival. Knowing that he would go to jail and fearful of retribution from her son if she told me he was hiding in the bedroom closet, she remained silent.

Tony, this was not the first time I responded to my intuition with success, nor was it the last. I could have told myself that I was imagining things, that I had looked in the house and had found no indication of problems. But I knew better than to place judgement values on my intuition; I had listened to it before and I had been right. Honoring intuition and respecting our fears catapults our ability to know. The ability to operate successfully within the predatory environment of Corrections is directly tied to the ability to honor intuition and fear without criticism or censure

Of course fear, like everything else in life, must be in balance or it is harmful. In the correctional environment, you cannot maintain a constant state of anxiety. To do so would diminish your ability to perceive real danger. Instead, you must be able to discern healthy fear from unwarranted/unhealthy fear.

IN THE CORRECTIONAL ENVIRONMENT, YOU CANNOT MAINTAIN A CONSTANT STATE OF ANXIETY. TO DO SO WOULD DIMINISH YOUR ABILITY TO PERCEIVE REAL DANGER.

I heard a man comment on the radio yesterday that most people trap themselves in cages of fear built on "what-ifs," which impose artificial limits on success. He captured the idea most succinctly. They go through life claiming that they are not afraid of anything when all of their actions are predicated on fear. They fear what others think; they fear failure; they fear competition and success; they fear their feelings and rejection; they fear for their health, their children; and they demonstrate extreme concerns for the security of their lives and their possessions. They even fear hard work! Fear drives your thinking; it controls your life especially if you deny it.

If on the other hand you listen to fear and respect it, your performance can actually improve. It acts as a motivator, such as the 140-pound weakling who becomes a body builder or an expert in karate. Fear is the motivation that makes others such as me succeed. Fear of rejection makes some go through the painful process of breast implants, face-lifts, penile implants, or other cosmetic surgeries. Fear keeps others trapped in the generational cycle of low self-esteem, violence, and poverty, which is the legacy of many of the inmates with whom you will come in contact. Fearful people feel the need to be overprotective, to own weapons and control others. Fear becomes such a part of many people that they think that it is normal. Until something happens that triggers some inner work in their lives, until they can really see and appreciate how fear drives or motivates their

actions, they will never be able to manage fear effectively.

And so, what is the point? How does fear and intuition impact you and your life in Corrections? Tony, the Department of Corrections is predicated on fear: The society's fears that demand the incarceration of certain types of criminals; the fear-driven inmates who act out in a million and one ways as a result of that fear; the frightened correctional professionals who refuse to admit they know fear. Fear/anxiety is a reality of life to the officer working his post hoping at a minimum that he or she can go home without some inmate with some obnoxious disease gassing them. Fear/anxiety is a reality of life for the warden, who must be confirmed by the legislature, respected by diverse special interest ethnic groups, and who must be able to account for every action within the institution. In my 16 years working within the department, I never heard fear acknowledged (it would be weak); nor were methods of coping with fear taught in any classroom I am of which I'm aware.

> IN MY 16 YEARS WORKING WITHIN THE DEPARTMENT, I NEVER HEARD FEAR ACKNOWLEDGED ...

The Department has post-traumatic incidence counselors who offer assistance after every major incident. But it is my understanding that while help is offered, many times there is an underlying message – that to accept help would be construed as "weak." Correctional employees are expected by their peers to swallow huge amounts of stress and that is injurious to the employee and, indirectly, to everyone they deal with on a regular basis.

Tony, I am convinced that if fear were acknowledged and if methods of coping with fear were taught within the system, the number of stress claims would fall and much of the officer aggression that has been so visible in the media would disappear.

While it is difficult to change an entrenched culture, you can sensitize yourself to healthy and unhealthy aspects of fear and avoid the ill effects that follow from not recognizing it. I suggest the following:

- **Listen to your inner voice.** Note your fear/anxiety and do not judge or censure your emotional responses. Follow and honor your intuition, see where it leads you. Track your responses in a log.

- **Research the work others have done on the subject, noting similarities and differences to your experiences.**

- **Observe your coworkers and the inmates; see how they react to fear/anxiety.**

- **Using your experience and knowledge as a springboard, talk with your peers and discuss their experiences.** Have they had intuitive "gut feelings" that have led to significant actions in their lives? How do they typically respond to the intuitive feelings? What do they think of fear? Of intuition? Do they honor and explore their feelings? Do they suppress the fear/anxiety, concerned that it may be perceived as weak or not logical? How does the correctional culture recognize and distinguish between healthy fear and unwarranted fear?

- **Develop an outline for a class on the subject and suggest it to your In Service Training Department.**

- **Read Gavin De Becker's book *The Gift of Fear,* which is an excellent book on the topic.**

WE DISCOVERED THAT MANY OTHERS ARE REDISCOVERING WHAT EARLY MAN KNEW, THAT EMOTIONAL INTELLIGENCE AND INTUITION ARE THE SPRINGBOARD TO TRUE INTELLIGENCE AND SUCCESSFUL LIVING.

Tony, in this letter we have defined fear and intuition and discussed the attributes of each in the correctional environment. We discovered that many others are rediscovering what early man knew, that emotional intelligence and intuition are the springboard to true intelligence and successful living. Consider engaging your peers in the discussion I suggest above; most important, increase your likelihood for a safe, healthy, and happy life, which is exactly what I want most for you. I love you, Tony.

Until next time,
Love, Mom

CHAPTER 7

Just Do Your Job;
Cars Break Down

November 21, 1999

Hi Son,

How are you? Are things going great? I am sure that they are! We have not heard much from you, so I assume that they keep you jumping from dawn until dusk. Nonetheless, you almost have this whipped. Graduation is just around the corner.

Everyone is fine here, busy as can be. The holidays are so hectic, but I love them. I love the feel of Christmas; everyone's generous spirit seems to emerge this time of year. We should have that generous spirit all year; this world would be a better place for it I assure you. In any event, I have been laughing to myself today because of a story I remembered that I want to share with you.

While working in Central Office as a Parole Agent III, Community Correctional Program Manager, Bob called me. I worked with Bob since I came into the system in 1982 and knew him quite well. I always found him interesting. He was very friendly, quite the socializer. He was "in the know." He had information about everything and everybody, and he didn't mind sharing it to his advantage. It was interesting to see Bob in action. As a strategist, he associated with just the right people, people who could be advantageous to his career. He worked the system to his advantage. He positioned himself and promoted through the ranks more on his connections than skills and ability. The guy spent more time as a mole, securing information and sharing it with strategic alliances, than he did doing his job.

They had a saying that applied to people like Bob when I worked within the institution that he was "in the car." Meaning he had aligned himself with people in authority and rode with them as they got promoted within the system. In choosing this tactic, he acquired a new family; his mentor became the parent, a dad in this case; the mentee played the "kid." Such behavior resembles that of the inmates, when a stronger inmate takes a youngster under his wing and offers protection in return for favors. The younger/weaker person always pays a price in terms of loyalty, work, dedication, silence, information and, in some cases, sexual favors.

This tactic has worked for many people. Many have successfully ridden on the coattails of others. But there is a danger inherent in relying solely on your ability to acquire information and aligning yourself with a person of power and authority and depending on that person to help you advance within the system. "Cars" break down, and when they do everyone in the car scrambles for another ride. Believe me, people are often left behind.

Another problem with being "in the car" is that you tend to make enemies. There are a lot of "cars" in Corrections. Each car competes for high stakes, and alignments with one car are often made at the expense of another. Not everyone reaches the goal. When one car wins, another loses; and, often bad feelings accompany the victory. Next time around the results may be quite different, and you never know when punishment may be meted out.

DO YOUR JOB WHOLEHEARTEDLY; THERE IS VALUE IN EVERY EXPERIENCE, EVEN IN THE MOST BORING POST IN THE INSTITUTION.

Now, what if you are "in the car" and the driver jumps out? This happens in many ways: retirement, promotions, demotions, etc. Suddenly you are on your own, dealing with the enemies from other cars. Whoops! You have a big problem, assigned to first watch in the most godforsaken post on the institution's grounds for the rest of your career or until the person you angered retires. If your driver has not left the system and, if you are lucky, maybe he or she will pull you up when they move. Take for example Bob's case – when his dad left the system, his world caved in. One day he called me and asked me what he should do. My response was, and Tony, remember this if you remember nothing else: just do your job and do it well; cars break down.

Do not just show up to work halfheartedly. Don't get complacent and self-satisfied with just putting in your hours. Do your job wholeheartedly; there is value in every experience, even in the most boring post in the institution. At some point in your career, you might have to orient and motivate a subordinate to be excellent at that post. Be the best that you can be; give 150 percent and more. Determine where you want to go within the system and garner the experience and education that will take you there. Volunteer to shadow a person in a position into

which you would like to be promoted. Ask questions; learn everything that you can. Trust me, people will notice and you will be promoted on merit. People who do their time by just showing up to work expect to be promoted on longevity. Relying on longevity is self-defeating. You place yourself in a position where your only value lies in the information that you can provide or the people with whom you are aligned.

I do not say that there is no merit in aligning yourself with others. Do find a mentor, but base your choice on that person's leadership qualities, ethics, skills, and abilities. Develop a contract up front that defines each person's role and expectations, then honor that contract. There is no quicker path to growth than an apprenticeship with a knowledgeable, seasoned person who is not only the best at what they do, but who knows how to successfully work within the system.

Over the years I have had several great mentors. Without them, I do not know if I would have been as successful as I have been. You must be careful, as well as discerning, when choosing a mentor, however. I made some mistakes along the path. Although some will argue there is as much to be learned from a negative experience as from a positive one, becoming involved in a nonproductive mentoring relationship can be counter-productive. Further, you will be known by the company you keep.

One mentoring relationship in which I was involved turned into a situation in which sexual favors were ultimately requested because the mentor felt as if they were owed and the terms of the contract were not clear up front. I did not know how to handle the relationship when it turned from mentoring to pursuing, but I eventually got out of the relationship without harming my career. I would like to say I got out of the relationship intact, but I wasn't. I was angry. I felt abused and bullied, and the effects of that experience followed me. I resigned from an organization and avoided situations that had once brought me pleasure because of this person's involvement. This man was connected; he had the ability to harm my career, and he had let me know he was not averse to doing so. Sexual harassment was not addressed in those years as it is now. I would have been the loser in a confrontation.

So what is the best way to learn the skills and abilities that will make you an excellent correctional employee, assisting you up that ladder of success? Let's review:

> THERE IS NO QUICKER PATH TO GROWTH THAN AN APPRENTICESHIP WITH A KNOWLEDGEABLE, SEASONED PERSON WHO IS NOT ONLY THE BEST AT WHAT THEY DO, BUT WHO KNOWS HOW TO SUCCESSFULLY WORK WITHIN THE SYSTEM.

• **Avoid Politics:** Politics is like a spider web, because you do not know how or to what the web is connected. You may think you have escaped the trap, only to find yourself deeper in the web.

• **Do your jobs to the best of your ability:** Corrections is an industry that needs intelligent, skilled, principled employees who know how to lead as well as follow.

• **Contract with a mentor:** Establish up-front the expectations for each party and go the distance. No one wants to mentor a half-willing employee.

• **Be discerning:** Question the motives and actions of others. Align yourself only with people of character and principles because these individuals will go the distance.

ALIGN YOURSELF ONLY WITH PEOPLE OF CHARACTER AND PRINCIPLES BECAUSE THESE INDIVIDUALS WILL GO THE DISTANCE.

I know that you are aware of a lot of this information, and this letter only serves as a reminder. For myself, many times a gentle reminder is in order. I love you and want to make sure you go into the institution well prepared. Take care and I will see you at graduation. Give me a call if there is anything I need to bring when I come down.

Lots of Love,
Mom

Modeling and Leadership

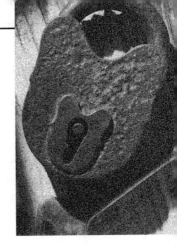

November 29, 1999

Dear Son:

How are you today? Getting a little tired or stressed maybe? Hang in there. This will be over fast, and you will look back on it with fond memories. I have just a quick question: Have they talked at all about leadership in the Academy? I would think so; leadership is the topic du jour in just about every publication that one reads. I do not know what they are telling you, but I have a few thoughts that I want to share with you.

There is a wealth of information available on the topic of leadership, just browse your local bookstore. Each book lists the qualities a particular author believes are important in a leader. Much of what I've read I call "feel-good" rhetoric. It really has not done anything to change people's lives. Further, given the difficult environment of Corrections, I do not know how much good a list of qualities will do for you when you are exposed to an inmate who has just stabbed a fellow officer and the anger surges through you urging retaliation. Or, when a group of your peers tries to pressure you to conform to behavior that your intuition tells you is wrong. You do not need a list of qualities, you need the tools to fight and fight fiercely to hang onto those standards and principles that act as your rudder in turbulent waters. Further, I do not know how well all these self-help books cultivate a reader's ability to lead. Maybe it's that many of the people I worked for in Corrections did not read enough about leadership.

Some administrators were very authoritarian; they led by command and control, by muscle, much as we have been taught to manage inmates. At the other end of the spectrum, some managed by consensus, but rarely achieved consensus, so consequently little ever got done. I have worked for poor managers and for great managers and,

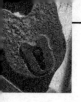

over years of observing management in practice, I have developed my own list of criteria, which I believe the most effective leaders in Corrections share.

In my mind, no one is more compelling than a confident person who is self-contained – a person with value and character, whose life and attitude reflect his/her beliefs. People are drawn to him or her like moths to a flame. Often, in describing such a person, it is difficult to articulate their source of power. It is not an external characteristic; it is an internal radiance that emanates from them. You might not recognize these people by the designer clothes that they wear or the car that they drive. You might not recognize them by their high status or long list of accomplishments. They distinguish themselves by virtue of their inner strength, which is evident in everything that they do.

... DEMONSTRATION AS OPPOSED TO VERBALIZATION THAT WILL ALLOW YOU TO INFLUENCE OTHERS. IN OTHER WORDS: ACTIONS SPEAKS LOUDER THAN WORDS.

They have the ability to enjoy life, thinking and acting based on values and moral guidelines rather than from fears based on past experiences. Armed with wisdom and common sense, they are not interested in judging themselves or others, and they seek solutions as opposed to reveling in conflict. Sensitive, compassionate, and empathetic, they have the ability to connect with others, inspiring in each person they touch a sense of self-worth and a desire to become the best. They communicate clearly and concisely, praising or challenging appropriately. They are quick to admit their own mistakes, allow others their failures, and acknowledge that even in mistakes, wisdom is gained. They are comfortable sharing the credit for success and they are not intimidated by the strengths of others. People with these characteristics are able to influence most people.

Do you know any people with these characteristics? They come immediately to mind because they are the ones who have had the most profound impact on your life. Many people talk about leadership today – it is a buzzword in every industry. There are many approaches to leadership and lots of good advice on how to cultivate the qualities of a good leader. Sometimes an article in a trade journal or an excellent motivational speaker will inspire others to achieve greatness. But, in most cases, it is the impact of a person with the aforementioned qualities that speaks to one's spirit and makes a difference. Tony, it is demonstration as opposed to verbalization that will allow you to influence others. In other words: actions speaks louder than words. You lead and you teach best by example. Ultimately, character in action is

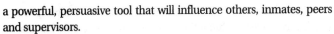

a powerful, persuasive tool that will influence others, inmates, peers and supervisors.

There is a hierarchy in Corrections; a chain of command structured around standard operating protocols that form the backbone of the system. Nonetheless, each person in the organization has the power to influence the system, either positively or negatively, regardless of classification or title. An administrator I worked for at the Correctional Medical Facility in Vacaville offers one example of such a person.

Two years into my tenure with the department, I was already jaded and cynical, tired of working with people who were slicker than most of the inmates. I was naïve initially, and was recruited "into the car" of an influential person. This person was a master of political games, adept at deceit and manipulation. He had both authority and connections; for example, he was on a first name basis with the Director of Corrections. He would position me on task forces or special assignments then manipulate the situation through me to suit his own purposes. On the exterior, he appeared charismatic and caring, which attracted people in droves. On the inside, however, he was different. He used his power and influence to make or break careers on whim. He was dangerous if crossed and did not hesitate to use his power to the detriment of others. I found that many in the institution were just like him. In fact I could sit in a meeting room and tell you who was the voice for other persons of influence. This was how the game was played and most of us accepted this as a fact of life. There was one administrator, however, who was different.

I SENSED IMMEDIATELY THAT HE WAS DIFFERENT. HE HAD A QUIET CONFIDENCE AND WORKED FROM HIS CORE OF VALUES.

I first met this person when I was assigned to a task force in which he was the lead. I sensed immediately that he was different. He had a quiet confidence and worked from his core of values. He was refreshingly honest and non-manipulative. He was the epitome of the characteristics I spoke to at the beginning of this letter. I was so impressed by the person, I decided that I wanted to emulate his style. He became a powerful influence, on my career and on the formation of my beliefs on power, influence and leadership. He taught me a valuable lesson.

If you want to influence the behavior of others, cultivate those behaviors in yourself first. It is just that simple. I have heard that only seven percent of what adults learn is from what they hear; a majority of what they learn is gleaned from what they observe and from their own experiences – what they discover for themselves. Most people believe what they see, and if they see the benefit of a certain type of a behavior as positive or effective, many will adopt that behavior. Millions of dollars in marketing is allocated on that premise. So what does this mean for you?

- **If you want to work with people who are wise, seek wisdom yourself.**

- **If you want to work with people who are empathetic and who work well with others, seek those characteristics for yourself.**

- **Do you value in others the ability to find solutions/resolutions to conflict? Master the skill yourself.**

- **Do you want others to listen to you? Learn to listen first.**

- **Do you value coworkers whose integrity you can trust, upon whom you can depend, who live by a set of standards? Cultivate those qualities.**

- **What kind of men do you want your sons to become? Be that man yourself.**

MOST PEOPLE BELIEVE WHAT THEY SEE, AND IF THEY SEE THE BENEFIT OF A CERTAIN TYPE OF A BEHAVIOR AS POSITIVE OR EFFECTIVE, MANY WILL ADOPT THAT BEHAVIOR.

Tony, every person plays many roles in life, sometimes you lead and sometimes you follow. Follow with discernment and lead by your convictions. Let your life and behavior speak for you. You will appear much more credible; inspire a loyal "Follower-ship™" and find an abundance of success in whatever role you pursue. Think about it.

I love you lots,
Mom

CHAPTER 9

Your Family as a Barometer

December 3, 1999

Hi Son,

I just got through talking to Kim. She is learning to problem solve, although she would rather have you available at least by phone for consultation. The kids miss you as well and they are proud of you. You have done a good job of preparing them for your time away. Anthony cracks me up; he is such a little man, opinionated and decisive for a seven-year-old. You do a good job with your family, and I am proud of you for that. So many people do not make their families a priority, which is a huge issue in Corrections.

I have heard that the divorce rate in Corrections is huge. I do not know of any statistic, but judging by the people I know, I believe it to be correct. That is horrible considering the trauma a divorce inflicts on families. Children who grow up without both parents are more likely to have significant problems. I heard on the radio this morning that a study coming out of Oakland, California, documents that 90 percent of those children involved in drugs, gangs, and street violence don't have their fathers in the home.

The value of family is immeasurable always, but when you become employed with the Department of Corrections, it is even more so. Your family can and should act as a barometer that helps you maintain a normal (or somewhat normal) perspective on the world. They knew you before, they share values, they will support you throughout your career, and they will be there for you when that career has ended. Depending upon your relationship, they will be honest with you about your behavior if it becomes skewed by the world of deviance you will be entering.

The love bond shared by two committed adults and the nurturing of your children will become powerful antidotes to the daily assault of negativism to which you will be subjected in Corrections. It is the reminders of the standards by which you live that anchor you when everything around you suggests that lessening of standards is permitted and encouraged.

You see Tony, as you spend more and more time behind the gates, you are exposed to the negativism much more than to a healthy approach to life. You become vulnerable to negatives insidious effects. What once appeared as obscene and deviant will begin to be accepted as routine, as a way of life, in fact, comedic. I know whereof I speak. I sometimes feel like a woman with a sick sense of humor, unaffected by many things that bother women outside of the Department. Your career in Corrections can and will negatively affect your family, and no career is worth that sacrifice. Trust me, when the chips fall, your family will be there for you, not the Department, as evidenced by my story.

I WORKED LONG HOURS, SOMETIMES FROM THREE OR FOUR IN THE MORNING UNTIL TEN AT NIGHT. I DID NOT SEE MY FAMILY, EXCEPT IN PASSING, AND WHEN I CAME HOME, I WAS TOO TIRED TO PAY ATTENTION.

It was Monday, February 16, 1998, around 11:30 in the morning. I had been having what I thought was indigestion all the prior week. My job was particularly stressful. The chain of command had broken down. I was a Parole Agent III, acting Parole Administrator of the Community Correctional Program unit. We had a new Parole Administrator II and a new Assistant to the Deputy Director. I was working on a program in which the Director's office held great interest. Getting instructions directly from the Director's office, I also received conflicting instructions from the new Assistant Deputy Director. I had no recourse, except to try and accommodate everyone's wishes, not an enviable position. I worked long hours, sometimes from three or four in the morning until ten at night. I did not see my family, except in passing, and when I came home, I was too tired to pay attention.

I thought that a little medication would ease my indigestion because whatever little stomach ailment I had was not leaving and I felt quite annoyed with it. I took some Maalox then decided to take a bath to see if I could relax.

I filled the tub with hot, sudsy water, added my favorite fragrance, and settled in for what I thought would be a calming experience. Was I ever wrong! The pain in my chest became intolerable. It felt like a bull, you know the kind the cowboys ride in the rodeo, bucking and heaving, heaving and bucking on my chest, and with each blow the pain grew more unbearable.

I quickly called my husband and told him that I was in serious trouble and to get home, which he did. He took me directly to the hospital. I was told later that that was a big mistake, that if I had gotten stuck in traffic, I could have died. I should have called 911, but I believe that I was still trying to deny that I had a serious problem.

Fear – I have never known such fear. You see, when I realized I was having a heart attack, I remembered that 50 percent of people who have heart attacks do not survive, and I did not want to die.

The minute I walked into the hospital, they knew I was in trouble. They rushed me back to the emergency room. They allowed John to stay with me and, during the attempt to save me with the tubes, the drugs, and the wires, and in the midst of horrible pain, I tried to tell my husband the things that I should have been telling him all along.

I told him what a good man he was and how much I respected him, his values, and what he had accomplished in his life. I told him I loved him and begged him to tell my family and my mother and sisters the same. I asked to him to tell Ivan and Kimberly that I loved them and thought of them always, and told him tell you that I loved you and your family as well. I asked him to let you guys know that you were in my heart and on my mind when I died. I continued to tell him these things until my heart stopped.

FEAR – I HAVE NEVER KNOWN SUCH FEAR. … I REMEMBERED THAT 50 PERCENT OF PEOPLE WHO HAVE HEART ATTACKS DO NOT SURVIVE, AND I DID NOT WANT TO DIE.

You know the rest of the story, how they were able to restart my heart, perform an angioplasty, insert a stint, and I am here today to tell you how to prevent the same from happening to you.

Tony, at no time during the entire event did I think of my career or the people at work. At no time during the incident was anyone at work with me; my family was my entire support. During the next few days, while lying in the hospital wondering if I was going to live or die, during the next months when I knew my career, my life, as I had known it was over, my family was my support. During that entire first agonizing year, as I redefined my existence, my family was always there.

Don't get me wrong, a large number of concerned people called and wished me well. I still maintain contact with some of them, those with whom I had developed significant relationships. But the big impersonal organization, the bureaucracy, threw me away as one would toss a used tissue. The organization to which I had devoted over sixteen years of my life, sixteen years in which I had dedicated myself to my career at the expense of my personal life, assumed the position

that I was dispensable, of no particular value. It made me very angry. It is a reality, however, that we assume we are important to the system, when in fact there are a variety of bright capable people waiting to take our place.

The point I am making is this Tony. Family is the most important thing in the world. When all is said and done, they will be there for you. Align yourself with them; listen to your family. Watch how they approach you. Be sensitive to their opinions and observations. Question any perceived weakening of the bonds you share and quickly resolve any problems. Let them know that they are most important part of your life. Spend quality time with them, reinforcing those beliefs, feelings, and values you hold most dear. Talk to them honestly about your concerns, and ask for their feedback and guidance. Use them as a barometer, and they will be true to you.

FAMILY IS THE MOST IMPORTANT THING IN THE WORLD. WHEN ALL IS SAID AND DONE, THEY WILL BE THERE FOR YOU.

My life changed in less than one minute. One minute is all it takes to turn your life around, ask Christopher Reeves. Do not let the career you have chosen negatively impact your relationship with your family. Be constantly vigilant so that your relationships are not polluted with the poison of the system. Listen to me, Tony, and you will avoid much of the stress and pain that others before you have suffered in their ignorance.

I know that you are getting bombarded with information and these are really heavy letters. Read them now and them put them away for a year. If you come back to them, see if I am not telling you the truth. See if I know whereof I speak. I love you and want you to be happy and to be spared any unnecessary pain.

See you soon,
Love, Mom

CHAPTER 10

The Danger in Complacency

December 5, 1999

Hey Buddy!

What is going on? Are you in better physical shape than you have been in for a while? I know you really like to condition yourself, and you know the value of a consistent exercise program. For goodness sake, stay that way! Don't laugh. Wait until you get to the institution, and you will see why I am concerned.

When you first start your career within the Department, you do not know what to expect, and fear is a great motivator. You hear the war stories and determine that you had better be in shape to manage the inmates. You hit the ground running, so to speak and, over the course of your first few years in corrections, you tend to stay in good physical condition. Many stay in great shape throughout their career.

Some, however, become complacent; why I do not know. Maybe they are assigned to a post that has not required any physical exertion, in which they feel somewhat secure, and they relax. Whatever the reason, they get comfortable.

Tony, the biggest danger in the institution is comfort and complacency (right up there with officers who purposefully agitate the inmates, risking themselves as well as the inmates). Many do their job the same way every day for years and nothing happens to them, so they let their guard down, but they still believe that they are on top of their job. That is when they are in the most danger.

Complacency leads a person to become less observant, it opens windows of opportunity for the inmates, plus it permits people to take less care of their health. The weight creeps up, they work out less and before you know it, they are 30 pounds overweight and a risk to everyone within the institution. Others do not gain weight, but they cease to do any aerobic conditioning or strength training, and they become

flaccid as a sloth, which is as equally as dangerous.

Just wait, you'll see them. You'll report to your post and meet a co-worker with a huge, ponderous gut, grinning at you, eating a donut. What happens if there is an incident, and you need back up? HELLO, do we work in the same place? They look like they would suffer a coronary if they had to sprint ten feet, and they might. Remember, I used to be a nurse in the institution. You would be amazed at how many officers I cared for who had health problems after sprinting to an alarm.

Such officers are frightening, and they are so self-absorbed they cannot see they are, in fact, a safety risk. I really believe that they think they still have it under control and feel they can handle any emergency that comes up. Not only are they hurting themselves, but also they are putting others at risk. What if they cannot perform? You are on your own! What if they fall out? Not only do you have to control a potentially dangerous situation, but you also have to worry about a fellow officer.

THE WORK IS PHYSICALLY DEMANDING AND, IF PEOPLE DO NOT STAY IN SHAPE, PROBLEMS CAN AND DO OCCUR.

I am not at all suggesting that it is okay to discriminate against people who are obese or out of condition. You know me; I would like to think that there is not a prejudiced bone in my body. I have nothing but concern. I am arguing, however, that the Department should do more to maintain health and safety standards. They do have a physical agility program that rewards those who are fit, but they need to go further. The work is physically demanding and, if people do not stay in shape, problems can and do occur. Let me tell you my story.

The site is early morning at B1 Clinic (B1 clinic is not the only post I ever worked, it just happens to be the source of a lot of stories). There were no correctional officers assigned to the clinic at that time, only another medical technical assistant and me. It was our task to perform the custody duties and manage medical concerns as well. Not a problem; we had been led to believe that we could manage the impossible and we were tough.

It was breakfast and the mainline released for chow. The clinic is situated right across from the chow hall, and there is a tremendous amount of inmate movement at that time. Many inmates will stop for their hot meds, insulin injections, sign up for sick call, or any other opportunity that availed itself. In any event, this day was like every other in many ways, with one exception: The Depend™ Moment!

Now before I go further into the story, I would like to preface it by saying that I think some correctional officers are blind. That's right, blind. I got proof that day. How else could a seven-foot tall, psychotic, bleeding Goliath get to the clinic without a call or an escort or some forewarning? He had to get off the tier and past a grill gate to get to the clinic. This was not a mouse, and I am not talking just a big guy, I am talking about someone almost larger than life.

You know that Vacaville is renowned for its psychiatric cases and this was one of them. This man walked into, or should I say tromped into, the clinic. Grunnnk! Grunnnk! The only reason we knew he was coming was the vibrations of the earth as he got closer. Grunnk! Grunnk! I thought we were having an earthquake, but it was the most unusual earthquake I had ever felt. By this time everyone knew there was something amiss and the clinic grew very quiet. Even the inmates stopped their incessant chatter.

The man was a site to behold. He sported a Mohawk, which he had shaved just that morning, as evidenced by the blood running in trickles down his face and neck. Not enough blood to suggest a serious head wound; we knew that wasn't a problem, just enough blood to make him look sinister. His clothing didn't help. He was barefoot with only a blanket, shaped as a loincloth around his groin: a behemoth with a bloody head in a giant loincloth. He was not something you see every day, not even in Vacaville. Have you seen movies where time seems to stand still? Time did stand still at that moment.

HE WAS BAREFOOT WITH ONLY A BLANKET, SHAPED AS A LOINCLOTH AROUND HIS GROIN: A BEHEMOTH WITH A BLOODY HEAD IN A GIANT LOINCLOTH.

Picture this, the clinic was filled with inmates and two of the puniest medical technical assistants on staff. I was all of 5'4" and 110 pounds, and my partner, well, my partner was punier than I was. No one can say that I am neither a trained observer nor a quick study. I took one look at Goliath, one look at my partner, and knew without a doubt that we were in deep stuff. Did you ever wish you didn't have to deal with something? I knew I did not want to deal with it because I said to myself, "Oh God, I don't want to deal with this!"

You learn things about yourself when you work the mainline. You learn not just all the flaws to which the inmates draw your attention, but you also find qualities you didn't know you had. I knew I had heart after that morning, because I gathered myself together and walked right up to that inmate. With all the courage I could muster, using all the psychiatric assessment skills I possessed and praying, I spoke right into his bellybutton.

God does answer prayers; the situation could have been much worse than it was. The man was psychotic, but not aggressive. He

responded well to me, and we got him treatment. I don't know about the blind officers. I suggested that they have their eyes examined, but they never got back to me.

Complacency reveals itself in many a dangerous way besides physical deterioration: prison riots, assaults, introduction of contraband, and a variety of other dangerous situations that could be avoided by alert, attuned staff.

So, how do you combat complacency? You work in a situation that requires teamwork; in fact, anything that happens to your brother or sister officers, also happens to you. Fight complacency as a team; motivate each other to stay in shape. If you are concerned about a coworker's physical condition, tell that person, challenge him or her. Set up scenarios in which you hide artificial contraband on each other's posts. Test their observation skills, and keep them keen. You are each other's safety net. The bottom line is, stay in shape, please! Do not become complacent. Consider eye examinations if you must, your life and the lives of your coworkers depend on it.

LISTEN TO YOUR BODY. LEARN TO IDENTIFY THE EFFECTS OF STRESS AND TAKE STEPS TO ELIMINATE OR REDUCE THOSE EFFECTS. IN THE LONG RUN, YOUR EFFORTS WILL PAY OFF IN HUGE DIVIDENDS.

Tony, there are other reasons that you must maintain your health through diet and exercise, and the most important reason is your ability to manage stress. The seven-foot inmate didn't take me out, yet the stress almost killed me. You must be as concerned about the stress as you are concerned about managing the inmates. There are so many people in denial, do not be one of them.

Stay attuned to your body. Listen to your body. Learn to identify the effects of stress and take steps to eliminate or reduce those effects. In the long run, your efforts will pay off in huge dividends.

A number of books available now teach you how to listen to your body. They explain the symptoms of stress and discuss behavioral approaches for managing stress-related symptoms. Invest in yourself; learn and share these techniques with your coworkers. You cannot rely on others to take care of your health; not even your doctor can help if you are not doing your part.

You are accountable for everything that happens to you in your life, including the status of your health. As soon as you believe that and take the steps necessary to protect yourself, you will have made major progress towards a happy, healthy, balanced life.

I love you!
Take Care, Mom

CHAPTER 11

Go and Be Safe

December 12, 1999

Hi Son,

Are you glad to be home and with your family? It probably feels a little strange after six weeks away. You will have your rhythm back in no time. I know you are anxious to report to the institution for your first day of work Monday, but relax, you already have everything you need to be successful.

Your instructors at the Academy were very conscientious, teaching you everything they knew to ensure you were prepared for this day. I hope my letters have armed you with information that will not only help you work successfully within the system, but also will help you to maintain your health, achieve a work/life balance, and maintain the integrity of your family. If you are able to accomplish these things, then I have achieved my goal of adequately motivating and preparing you.

Your graduation ceremony affected me in a number of ways. First I am very proud of you and your accomplishments. Beyond that, it helped me close a chapter in my own life. Leaving the system as I did with the heart attack, I had not been able to bring closure to that part of my life. Your graduation ceremony helped me with that. It was as if I were passing the torch to a new generation. One of your presenters was a gentleman with whom I had worked when I entered the system, and his announcement of retirement reestablished the fact that there is a time and season for everything, and that my time in Corrections was over.

I worked for the Department of Corrections for 16 of the most rewarding years of my life. I worked with some of the bravest, finest, most caring professionals I have ever known. I have had the privilege of watching inmates who appeared to have no hope, turn their lives

around. I have had an impact. I made a difference. Sixteen years went very quickly, and they will for you as well. Where does the time go?

Tony, I wish you success, balance, and happiness. May your career be purposeful, challenging, and safe. What you do is tremendously important. You have the power to impact lives; do not abuse or take that power lightly. It is an awesome responsibility. One day, when you leave the system, and if I have done my job well, you will leave the system after a long career through a traditional retirement. I want you to be able to look back with pride, knowing that you did your job with professionalism and integrity, that you are part of a family of professionals who help keep our communities secure. I know I do.

I love you,
Mom

YOU HAVE THE POWER

TO IMPACT LIVES;

DO NOT ABUSE OR TAKE

THAT POWER LIGHTLY.

P.S. I have attached a list of books that have been very helpful to me over the years. You may also find them useful in your life and in your career.

Suggested Reading List

BOOKS

Arendt, Hannah. *Eichman in Jerusalem - A Report on the Banality of Evil.*
New York, Penguin Books, 1963

Clark, Walter Van Tilburg. *The Ox-Bow Incident.*
New York, Penguin Group, 1940

Cooper, Robert K. and Sawaf, Ayman. *Executive E.Q..*
New York, Grosset/Putman, 1997

DeBecker, Gavin. *The Gift of Fear.*
New York, Del Publishing, 1997

Gallagher, Winifred. *The Power of Place.*
New York, HarperCollins, 1993

Harvey, Jerry B. *The Abilene Paradox.*
San Francisco, Josey Bass Publishing, 1988

Kalinich, David B. and Pitcher, Terry. *Surviving in Corrections.*
Springfield, Charles C. Thomas, 1984

Segal, Jeanne. *Raising Your Emotional Intelligence.*
New York, Henry Holt and Company, 1997

Seligman, Martin E.P. *What You Can Change...And What You Can't.*
New York, Ballantine Books, 1993

Thayer, Robert E. *The Origin of Everyday Moods.*
New York, Oxford University Press, 1996

TAPES

Goldman, Daniel. *Emotional Intelligence.*
Los Angeles, Audio Renaissance Tapes, 1995

Acknowledgements

This book would not have been possible without the relationships, experiences, and insights developed during my journey through the correctional maze. Thank you, each and every one of you, for touching my life.

With loving gratitude to both of my sons – their experiences within the correctional system helped shape my perceptions and were the inspiration for this book.

China and Muni, your contributions and insights are greatly appreciated.

A hats off to my husband whose amazing patience allowed him to listen, listen, and listen to every idea.

My special thanks to Maureen Jung, the writing guru, whose insight, solid advice, and encouragement in times of doubt led to the conclusion of this project. I could not have done it without her!

Finally, to Laurel and LeeAnn at Mystic Design, Inc. whose wit, excellent graphic design skills, direction, and support kept me moving, a huge thank you! You have always gone the extra mile!

Notes